The High Calling of God

A Look At The Bride of Christ

Philippians 3:13-14

Brethren, I count not myself to have apprehended: but this one thing I do, forgetting
those things which are behind, and reaching forth unto those things which are before, I press toward the mark for the prize of the high calling of God in Christ Jesus.

A Doctrinal Examination By:

Dennis R. Wharton

Produced by Dennis Wharton
Redding, Ca. 96002

DennisWharton.com

Dedication:

To My Special Wife Linda who was my constant helper and encourager. She is a doctrinally and spiritually deep woman giving me valuable insights through the editing process. In the many Areas where my skills lacked she was there dedicating her time to help me.

To my mentor and Special friend Larry Crouch and his Wonderful wife Joyce for all of their guidance along the road to the completion of this book. Pastor Crouch added much of his knowledge on this subject of the Bride to expand my thinking as the story came together.

The High Calling of God

A Look At The Bride of Christ

A doctrinal observation

Dennis R. Wharton

FORWARD

It is an honor and privilege to be asked by the author of this book to write a brief forward. I have personally known the author for some fifty years. I count him as one of my dearest friends. I have found him to be a caring and compassionate pastor and a man who stands up boldly for the truth of God's Word.

The subject he has chosen for this book should be of great importance to every believer, because it is of great importance to God. The New Testament Church will endure throughout all the ages as the Bride of Christ. In the Western culture the focus at weddings is always on the bride, but in Biblical times, and in the wedding planned by our Heavenly Father, the focus will be on the Groom, Jesus Christ and the Bride's relationship to Him.

There are several unique things about this book. Having had the privilege of reading the manuscripts ahead of publication, I was first taken by the writer's approach to the subject as only he could do. When I finished one chapter I anxiously awaited the next chapter to see what was to be revealed on the next page. Another unique thing about this book is the fact that it meets the need of the theologian, teacher, church member or your average reader. The writer proves to have a good grasp of his subject and Bible doctrine. This will help the pastor prepare messages, the teacher prepare lessons and the church member to be stronger in the faith.

Brother Dennis Wharton has proven himself as a faithful pastor and teacher. He has made some wonderful contributions to the Churches of California through Bible Seminars, Missions and Church Camp. I believe that this book, when properly read and studied, will prove one of his greatest contributions. He has the courage to stand and present the truth of God's Word with zeal and compassion. Brother Wharton has suffered several serious health problems that have hindered him some physically, however, spiritually he remains strong in the service of the Lord.

A suggestion: As you read this book, you will be tempted to turn to the last chapters. DON'T do it! Read and absorb each line, paragraph and page before turning to the next. Be certain you have fed and digested each and every truth before you finally get to the dessert.

By His Grace:

Pastor: Larry W. Crouch

Landmark Missionary Baptist Church

Oakhurst, California

One

BRIDE INTRODUCTION

I have entitled this book *The High Calling*. My hope is that all who read it will consider the Almighty, God-given, and sovereign truth that God—who made this world and all that is in it—on the sixth day created a being whom He desired would ascend to the highest pinnacle of success. The being, Adam, did not reach that goal in his early years. However, God's eternal plan and purpose for him and his posterity were not altered by Adam's fall. God already had a plan in place for the redemption of Adam and all mankind. It involved the shedding of innocent blood. This happened so that a sin-cursed creation could once again come into a relationship with the God of creation. Thus, ultimately attaining to the "High Calling."

Similar to God's desire for His children, we, as finite beings have great desires and hopes for our children when they are born into this world. We look at their innocence in the crib, and we consider what we would like their futures to be. Of course, we want the very best for them: good health, freedom from physical deterrents and to be unblemished so others will like and treat them well. Our desires are for them to have an intelligence that will make learning and advancement uncomplicated. We also desire an education that will take them to the highest levels of academia with degrees that will set them apart from others. Possibly, they will write the textbooks that others use to acquire an education.

Physically, we want them to excel so they will be the popular athletes from grade school through to their university years. Maybe, they will show their excellence at the World Olympics receiving more gold medals than anyone who went before. Furthermore, we want them to excel in the social world as well, maybe even advancing in the political world. Perhaps, he or she would become a governor, senator, or president. Do you suppose? Our children will not become any of those delinquents who end up in jail or "dead-beat" dads who will not care for their families.

Realizing we have mentally had this conversation standing over our sleeping babies, who cannot even change their dirty diapers, causes us to realize we have no control over any of these circumstances. On the other hand, God our Father has great desires for the future of His children and He, unlike us does have the power to offer us the best future.

This book *The High Calling of God* will deal with God's desire to move us from the cradle, (born again,) to the "ultimate prize" in the Christian life. No greater privilege is afforded the child of God than to be married to the Son of God, Jesus Christ! The "High Calling" is the opportunity to live eternally with Jesus, the bridegroom, in the New Jerusalem as His bride. He has gone to prepare a mansion for His bride that overshadows all the great wonders of the world ever seen or known by man. From the Scriptures, we will discover that this is not something automatically received at our birth into God's family. It is my hope that you will take the time to read this book and research the Scriptures. Prayerfully, this will enable you to see that God does have an "ultimate prize," which He desires to give to all of His children.

Philippians 3:13, 14, *"Brethren, I count not myself to have apprehended: but this one thing I do, forgetting those things which are behind, and reaching forth unto those things which are before, I press toward the mark for the prize of the high calling of God in Christ Jesus."*

Two

WHO IS THIS BRIDE?

Much controversy exists in the biblical world as to the identity of the bride of Christ. However, we won't find the answer to who she is by an examination of the creeds or doctrinal confessions of the different denominations of the religious world. That would only add more confusion to the mix. Ultimately, the answer will come from the inspired information God has provided us in the Bible. In this book, we will examine scriptures that mention or reveal the existence of such an entity. We will also consider scriptures that suggest the existence of a bride but do not use the name. Realizing that in many instances the differences in theological positions come from poor contextual renderings, we will pay strict attention to context.

Many born again children of God when asked what they believe the Bible teaches about the bride of Christ, will respond: "I don't know much about it." That has led me to believe that this doctrine (teaching) is not being preached from pulpits or taught in classes. *2 Timothy 3:16-17, "All scripture is given by inspiration of God, and is profitable for doctrine, for reproof, for correction, for instruction in righteousness: That the man of God may be perfect, throughly furnished unto all good works."* If being a part of the bride of Christ is the ultimate prize, then finding out who she is and how we might be part of her seems to be of great importance.

Some of the misunderstandings on this subject may come from *Revelation 19:1-9:*

> *And after these things I heard a great voice of much people in heaven, saying, Alleluia; Salvation, and glory, and honour, and power, unto the Lord our God: For true and righteous are his judgments: for he hath judged the great whore, which did corrupt the earth with her fornication, and hath avenged the blood of his servants at her hand. And again they said, Alleluia. And her smoke rose up for ever and ever. And the four and twenty elders and the four beasts fell down and worshipped God that sat on the throne, saying, Amen; Alleluia. And a voice came out of the throne, saying, Praise our God, all ye his servants, and ye that fear him, both small and great. And I heard as it were the voice of a great multitude, and as the voice of many waters, and as the voice of mighty thunderings, saying, Alleluia: for the Lord God omnipotent reigneth. Let us be glad and rejoice, and give honour to him: for the marriage of the Lamb is come, and his wife hath made*

herself ready. And to her was granted that she should
be arrayed in fine linen, clean and white: for the fine
linen is the righteousness of saints. And he saith unto
me, Write, Blessed are they which are called unto the
marriage supper of the Lamb. And he saith unto me,
These are the true sayings of God. (Revelation 19:1-9)

Actually, these scriptures reveal a great deal about the marriage of Jesus Christ to His bride. First, the location of the marriage is revealed in verse one, *"And after these things I heard a great voice of much people in heaven, saying, Alleluia; Salvation, and glory, and honour, and power, unto the Lord our God: "* The marriage is going to take place in heaven. This would be just prior to Jesus coming to the earth with all of His saints to establish a thousand-year reign here on planet Earth.

Next, we learn that God the Father will be exalted by the inhabitants of heaven. Verse four, *"And the four and twenty elders and the four beasts fell down and worshipped God that sat on the throne, saying, Amen; Alleluia."* Verses four and five show the excitement of all the inhabitants of heaven thundering their voices and their songs to exalt the sovereign God of creation because His Son is about to marry His bride. Adam and Eve, Moses, Abraham and Sarah, Joshua, Gideon, and the faithful mentioned in Hebrews the eleventh chapter are all there for Messiah is about to take His bride.

Three

What's The Big Deal?

"I don't get it? I've been saved for years and I've never heard my pastor preach about the bride of Christ. I can't remember one bible study where we discussed this topic. Why are you making such a big deal about it?" Surprisingly, this is not an uncommon response from born again children of God when you present the bride of Christ as a cardinal doctrine of the faith.

The book of Matthew, the twenty-second chapter tells a story about a king who prepared a great feast for his son's wedding. Many were invited to come and take part in that wedding, but they were all busy and did not think it worthy of their time or consideration. The king was greatly disturbed; those invited didn't seem interested in his son's wedding. Much discussion could be had about what the teaching of the parable is, but it will not take much reasoning on our part to understand why a king would be upset because no one was interested in his son's marriage. This is one of those events where we could put ourselves in the king's shoes and quickly understand how we would feel in similar circumstances.

 Does the Bible teach that Jesus is the Son of the King of kings? We should be able to get a quick positive response to that question. *John, 20:31 "But these are written, that ye might believe that Jesus is the Christ, the Son of God; and that believing ye might have life through his name."* Does the Bible teach that Jesus, the Son of God, (The King of kings) is going to marry a bride whom He will live with throughout eternity? Again, a positive response should be in order. *Revelation, 19:7-9 "Let us be glad and rejoice, and give honour to him: for the marriage of the Lamb is come, and his wife hath made herself ready. And to her was granted that she should be arrayed in fine linen, clean and white: for the fine linen is the righteousness of saints. And he saith unto me, Write, Blessed are they which are called unto the marriage supper of the Lamb. And he saith unto me, These are the true sayings of God."* There are several more revealing bits of information that the Bible presents about the marriage of God's Son that we will consider in greater depth in later chapters. At this point, we should have enough information to answer the question: "What's the big deal?"

 I am always surprised when I meet fellow brothers and sisters in Christ who have never learned much about the amazing benefits of being part of the bride of Christ. Most respond with something like: "I have never studied much about it, but it seems like I have heard that all who have repented and believed on the Lord Jesus Christ as their Savior will be a part of it." Even if it was a done deal, you would think that something as important as the marriage of the God of creation's only begotten Son would be especially interesting to know more about! Especially if we were going to be part of the bride He marries! One of my hopes in writing this book is that all who read it might get a glimpse of what being a part of this bride might look like!

Four
What Would It Look Like?

If we could take a tour of the new heaven and new earth, what would we see? Our conclusions from the last chapter, "What's the Big Deal?" were: If it's the marriage of God's Son, we ought to have some interest in it. Let's see if we can get some idea of what the eternal ages will look like.

In John, the thirteenth chapter, Jesus told His disciples that He was going to leave them. He was talking about His soon to be crucifixion, burial, and resurrection. He also told Peter that he would deny Him. In these verses, the whole group is pretty discouraged.

When Jesus saw how upset they were about what He said, He encouraged them with some information about their future residence with Him. They, along with all of us who read the chapter of John 14 learned something new.

> *Let not your heart be troubled: ye believe in God, believe also in me. In my Father's house are many mansions: if it were not so, I would have told you. I go to prepare a place for you. And if I go and prepare a place for you, I will*

come again, and receive you unto myself; that where I am, there ye may be also. (John 14:1-3)

Reading from Genesis all the way through the Old Testament, we are excited to know that God has special dwelling places for all of His children in heaven. In Jesus' words of encouragement to His disciples. He told them there are many mansions, (dwelling places) in God's house. Next, He told them something that was never revealed before: "I go to prepare a place for you!" The bridegroom told the espoused bride: "I'm going to prepare a special dwelling place for us to live." He further says, that He is coming back for her and is going to receive her unto Himself. They will live together in this mansion He has built. Are these disciples the *Bride?* These are the same disciples He has identified as His church in *Matthew, 16:18-20 "And I say also unto thee, That thou art Peter, and upon this rock I will build my church; and the gates of hell shall not prevail against it. And I will give unto thee the keys of the kingdom of heaven: and whatsoever thou shalt bind on earth shall be bound in heaven: and whatsoever thou shalt loose on earth shall be loosed in heaven. Then charged he his disciples that they should tell no man that he was Jesus the Christ."* Furthermore, when questioned about why His disciples did not fast, Jesus revealed them as His bride. *Matthew, 9:14-15 "Then came to him the disciples of John, saying, Why do we and the Pharisees fast oft, but thy disciples fast not? And Jesus said unto them, Can the children of the bridechamber mourn, as long as the bridegroom is with them? but the days will come, when the bridegroom shall be taken from them, and then shall they fast."*

Now that we know that Jesus Christ, the Son of God left Earth to prepare a special home for His bride, our interests should be peaked. Is there any information about this mansion He has gone to prepare? The answer to that question is yes, but we will have to search the Scriptures to find out more!

We are going to take a tour through the future "eternal ages" to see what things look like. We will need a tour guide, and I think—we might enlist an angel for that job. As John wrote the book of Revelation an angel came and showed him the special place where Jesus had gone to prepare for His bride.

> *And there came unto me one of the seven angels which had the seven vials full of the seven last plagues, and talked with me, saying, Come hither, I will shew thee the bride, the Lamb's wife. And he carried me away in the spirit to a great and high mountain, and shewed me that great city, the holy Jerusalem, descending out of heaven from God, Having the glory of God: and her light was like unto a stone most precious, even like a jasper stone, clear as crystal; (Revelation 21:9-11)*

Our trip looking at the final ages of God's eternal world will be imaginary, but it won't be fictional because we will look at the information the Bible gives us.

Disclaimer:

This is a non-fiction book. Some unorthodox methods are being used to open our thinking on a serious subject. We know that angels are not going to assume the role of "tour guides." Examining what the Scriptures say about the "pearly" gates does not offer the size of those pearls. We would assume that they must be quite large as kings will pass through the openings where they are set.

We are not given exact information concerning the appearance of the entrance to the city, but we do know it passes through the exterior wall. Because we know the width of the wall, we can make some assumptions about how it might appear. According to Scripture, it is covered in gold and the golden streets of the city come up to it.

Occasionally, I will describe how I think something looks using my imagination, not having a scripture that says it. My intention in doing this is to open our minds to see the glory of what God is offering to His faithful children. This will be happening mainly in these introductory chapters where we are trying to get a glimpse of the vastness and beauty of God's eternal ages. As we progress into the later chapters, we will be purely analyzing the Scriptures. My hope is that you will enjoy the journey.

The Journey

For us to take this trip, we will have to acknowledge some facts concerning our examination. First, we understand that we will be looking at spiritual things in a spiritual world, and we will be doing so in our human bodies with all of our frailties. If we were to take such a trip, in reality, we would have new glorified bodies. They would be sinless, they would not get tired, and they would not need food. We will take this trip in a heavenly bus, no need for fuel stops, no worries of flat tires—it might even be some kind of hovercraft, (let's make it a convertible so we don't miss anything). Now, in reality, we know that in the eternal ages, our travel will no doubt be by instant transfers to wherever we choose to be, but for our examination, we want to travel a little slower so we can take in all the sights. I trust you will bear with me in this folly, as I know it seems a bit ridiculous that we could enlist an angel's help and that we could take an imaginary trip into the future. Often in gospel music, we enter the realms of a dream, ("I dreamed of a city called Glory..." etc.). We do this to get a glimpse of eternal things. I trust you will see the value of our trip as we move on.

 In our new bodies, we will be in tune to see the spiritual things without the earthy things cluttering our minds or views. 1 John 2:16-17: *"For all that is in the world, the lust of the flesh, and the lust of the eyes, and the pride of life, is not of the Father, but is of the world. And the world passeth away, and the lust thereof: but he that doeth the will of God abideth for ever."* All of our senses will be purified: sight, smell, hearing, touch, and taste. Our thinking and our attitudes will be heightened because we will be filled with the fruits of the Spirit. Galatians 5:22-23: *"But the fruit of the Spirit is love, joy, peace, longsuffering, gentleness, goodness, faith, Meekness, temperance: against such there is no law."* If you have ever gone on a bus tour here in our real world you know how much better the trip would have been if all the passengers had possessed these fruits.

Our journey will take several days. We won't be stopping at night for there is no night there. We will not need hotels or restaurants to give us rest or nourishment. We won't need frequent stops in order to stretch our bones or muscles. The trip will not be burdensome or oppressive; it will be fun and exciting. We will be allowed for this short journey to experience what it will be like to be in a *heavenly body.* We will actually be in our human bodies but we will be allowed to take this trip without the need for food or bathroom trips. There will be places we won't be able to go because of our human forms. Here is what we will be doing. We will see the new heaven and new earth come down to earth and be permanently placed. We will see the walls and the foundation and the gates will be examined closely. The material used inside and outside of this special mansion that Jesus has prepared for His bride will be considered. The trees, the river, the lighting, and the throne will all be observed. This should be an informative and fun trip. I hope you enjoy the journey!

Five

Day One

Morning

We have gathered at our tour bus, having been met by our angelic guide. He begins our tour by pointing out that the earth is very different from what we have been used to seeing. As a matter of fact, the entire earth has been totally renovated by fire. All evidence of sin and the curse are gone—it's a brand new world. The exterior surface is completely changed. Everything that sin had brought into existence— the thorns and thistles, disease, germs, insect/pests, etc. have been destroyed *completely:*

But the heavens and the earth, which are now, by the same word are kept in store, reserved unto fire against the day of judgment and perdition of ungodly men. But, beloved, be not ignorant of this one thing, that one day is with the Lord as a thousand years, and a thousand years as one day. The Lord is not slack concerning his promise, as some men count slackness; but is longsuffering to us-ward, not willing that any should perish, but that all should come to repentance. But the day of the Lord will come as a thief in the night; in the which the heavens shall pass away with a great noise, and the elements shall melt with fervent heat, the earth also and the works that are therein shall be burned up. (2 Peter 3:7-10)

Furthermore, the oceans and seas have disappeared. Revelation 21:1: *"And I saw a new heaven and a new earth: for the first heaven and the first earth were passed away; and there was no more sea."* Of course, we are absolutely startled by what we see because we are looking at the earth in its cleansed state just prior to seeing the new heaven and the new earth come down from the sky. But—something else is missing! Our tour begins in the dark, that's right—the sun and the moon have also disappeared. Revelation 21:23: *"And the city had no need of the sun, neither of the moon, to shine in it: for the glory of God did lighten it, and the Lamb is the light thereof."*

Something else beyond our comprehension is about to take place as our guide directs our attention to the sky. Is that a light? It almost looks like a star. As we focus our attention upward, the huge light appears to be getting even bigger and is headed for the earth—it is moving straight toward us. As we are in our **human bodies**, we are stricken by fear just like John in the Book of Revelation when Jesus began to reveal these future events to him. Revelation 1:17 *"And when I saw him, I fell at his feet as dead. And he laid his right hand upon me, saying unto me, Fear not; I am the first and the last:"*

As this light gets closer, what we see is a 1,500 mile square cube. Our guide has set our tour bus right at one of the corners of this giant cube, and it looks like it will crush us. When it has set itself on the earth and our screams have subsided, our angel guide assures us that we have nothing to fear, he will keep us from harm as we continue our excursion. Finally, we settle down and stare in amazement at what we are seeing. We are at the southwest corner of the New Jerusalem.

We are in awe of the beautiful lights which bathes us. None of us has ever seen light like this and the amazing mixtures of colors are beyond comprehension. Our angelic guide sees our wonderment and informs us that he will give a more detailed explanation of the light as we travel a little further on our journey. The angel further reveals, you have just witnessed the placing of the New Jerusalem on the newly renovated earth. Because we are sitting at the bottom corner of this enormous structure we are able to view the western and southern walls. We are also able to look up to view the height, it just keeps going up, there seems to be no end. We get a similar feeling as we view the south and west walls; they just keep going, their end is not in sight.

Our guide calms us by saying, "You are all the children of the sovereign, mighty God of all eternity. He loves you so much, He was willing to let His creation crucify His Only Begotten Son on a cross so you could become His sons and daughters. He knows that some of the things you'll see will seem overwhelming, but He wants you to not fear because He will protect you. These are things you need to see. He wants you to have some idea of what He has in store for those who love Him.

"This city that you have just witnessed being planted is the place your Savior said He was going to prepare for His wife. This is the place where the two of them will live throughout eternity. It's pretty amazing wouldn't you say?" We just nod our heads in unison as he continues his narration of what we are seeing. "Most of the information I will be sharing with you on this tour will be about things you have already read about in your owner's manual, the Bible, but I will be directing your attention to the locations.

"Let's talk about the size of this city." Revelation 21:15-16: *"And he that talked with me had a golden reed to measure the city, and the gates thereof, and the wall thereof. And the city lieth foursquare, and the length is as large as the breadth: and he measured the city with the reed, twelve thousand furlongs. The length and the breadth and the height of it are equal."* "I know most of you on this tour are accustom to using U.S. standard measurements, so my information will be given in that form. A furlong is an eighth of a mile, which makes the length, width, and height of this mansion 1,500 miles. As you are looking down that west wall you will have to go 1,500 miles to the north corner. The same is true looking back to our right, the length of this southern wall is 1,500 miles to the east corner. Looking straight up from where we sit, the top of this building is 1,500 miles up. At each corner, we will find the same thing to be true.

"Therefore, as the city came down from the heavens you saw something that was massive but your human eyes did not allow you to exactly grasp what you were seeing. I believe the mathematical term would be a 'cube.' In your owner's manual, it is called a city that lieth foursquare. During your lifetime on earth, you never saw anything like this. Had all of the engineers that existed on earth gotten together, they could never have engineered such a structure.

"The square footage of the building is a staggering amount. The bottom floor of this city is 2,225,000 square miles. Yes, that is square miles and not square feet. And yes, that is million with a 'M'. The total interior structure is 3,375,000,000 cubic **miles**. The placement of this city is on the land mass that God promised to Abraham in the Old Testament. This is one of the reasons this city is called the New Jerusalem. It is the light source for the entire world:

And I saw no temple therein: for the Lord God Almighty and the Lamb are the temple of it. And the city had no need of the sun, neither of the moon, to shine in it: for the glory of God did lighten it, and the Lamb is the light thereof. And the nations of them which are saved shall walk in the light of it: and the kings of the earth do bring their glory and honour into it. (Revelation 21:22-24)

"On our tour, we will be stopping along the way to examine the beauty of the light coming out of the city. The outer wall is made up of precious stones, each with different colors and facets that create a combination of colors that make the light so beautiful. When we get to those stopping destinations, I will describe each of the stones and some of their special attributes. During your time on earth, you often marveled at the astonishing sunsets and sunrises and would comment on what a great artist God is. Those who traveled to places where they could see the aurora borealis were also amazed at the God who made such fascinating colors and the beauty of His creation. The walls, jewels, and stones that create them are the final exhibits of God's artistry.

"There are many other things I could point out while we are here at the corner of this great city, but we have many stops ahead of us. So we will continue on to those destinations with anticipation concerning those things God has prepared for them who love Him. Let's all get settled into our seats as we take off on a journey like you have never seen before."

Six

Day One – Noon

We haven't traveled very far down the road— and our guide stops the bus. He talks about the wall around this great city. Everyone in the bus is captivated by the awesome array of colors coming out of it. Before he begins to tell us about the wall, one of our passengers asks him a question about the height of the city. "You said the city is a 1500-mile cube, doesn't that put the top of it in outer space?" Our angel guide smiles, he knows that with our finite human minds, we could not fathom such distance, so he tries to put a human perspective on what we are seeing. "In the world where you live the statue of Liberty is 151 feet high, the Empire State Building, is 1,250 feet high. Mount Everest is about 29,000 feet, which is about five and a half miles high, much shorter than our 1,500-mile high city. Most jet airliners fly around 35,000 feet about seven miles up in the sky.

"You have to go up to about 62 miles to get into outer space. The space shuttles have flown as high as 400 miles and that's still short of the top of the New Jerusalem. You don't have to worry about the space station or satellites running into it because as I mentioned when we began our journey, the earth has changed. We no longer have a sun, moon, or stars, and the skies have been cleared out for the new eternal ages. Don't be concerned about the inhabitants having breathing problems as they go up into the upper portions of this new city. First of all, the new inhabitants have new bodies and secondly, God has a new 'climate control' system. The sun is no longer regulating earth's temperatures; God and His "new system" are controlling them. So, in answer to your question about the top of the city being in outer space, yes, it is in what you would call 'outer space' in the old world, but things are different here.

"No doubt, many of you are wondering how such a huge object—this new city, could be attached to our earth and not cause the planet's rotation to be off-kilter. It's probably time for me to give you a disclaimer about the kinds of information I will be able to share with you on our journey. You have heard the response of people who couldn't reveal information—'That's above my pay-grade.' There will be questions you will ask that I can't answer. The things I will share with you can be found in the Bible, and I will be careful to not answer things 'above my pay-grade.'

"Ok, we stopped here to talk about this astounding wall around the city. As you can see, it surrounds the whole city and is without breaks with the exception of the twelve gates. We will talk more about the gates on our next stop. Let's look at the scripture verses from the Bible that give the technical information about the walls":

And he measured the wall thereof, an hundred and forty and four cubits, according to the measure of a man, that is, of the angel. And the building of the wall of it was of jasper: and the city was pure gold, like unto clear glass. And the foundations of the wall of the city were garnished with all manner of precious stones. The first foundation was jasper; the second, sapphire; the third, a chalcedony; the fourth, an emerald; The fifth, sardonyx; the sixth, sardius; the seventh, chrysolite; the eighth, beryl; the ninth, a topaz; the tenth, a chrysoprasus; the eleventh, a jacinth; the twelfth, an amethyst. (Revelation 21:17-20)

"The first thing we notice is the width of the wall. It is 216 feet. A cubit is eighteen inches thus 1.5 feet times 144 is 216 ft. The height of the wall isn't as clear."

And he carried me away in the spirit to a great and high mountain, and shewed me that great city, the holy Jerusalem, descending out of heaven from God, Having the glory of God: and her light was like unto a stone most precious, even like a jasper stone, clear as crystal; And had a wall great and high, and had twelve gates, and at the gates twelve angels, and names written thereon, which are the names of the twelve tribes of the children of Israel: (Revelation 21:10-12)

"The scripture in verse 12 says the wall was 'great and high,....' And as you can see it is pretty high. Whether the wall is the same height as the width, I will let you decide. A 19 to 20-story building would be approximately 216 feet tall.

"The foundations of this wall are pretty spectacular as well. Here is what the Bible tells us:"

> *And the building of the wall of it was of jasper: and the city was pure gold, like unto clear glass. And the foundations of the wall of the city were garnished with all manner of precious stones. The first foundation was jasper; the second, sapphire; the third, a chalcedony; the fourth, an emerald; The fifth, sardonyx; the sixth, sardius; the seventh, chrysolite; the eighth, beryl; the ninth, a topaz; the tenth, a chrysoprasus; the eleventh, a jacinth; the twelfth, an amethyst. (Revelation 21:18-20)*

"The beauty of the lights we see emanating from the New Jerusalem comes from the Lamb of God, the Lord Jesus Christ passing through the foundation stones. As these magnificent colors fuse, they produce lights that have *never* been seen before. The reason they are different is because the light is passing from the inside out and it is coming from Jesus!

"There are specific colors with each of these foundations and each foundation has the name of one of the twelve apostles." Revelation 21:14: *"And the wall of the city had twelve foundations, and in them the names of the twelve apostles of the Lamb."* "Collectively, the twelve apostles represent the church that Jesus established during His personal ministry on earth. When light passes through each of these precious stones, they produce multiple arrays of colors. The first foundation stone is jasper, which can be red, brown, reddish-brown, or yellow in color. The 6,000 mile- long wall is made of this stone and the face-to-face beauty of this stone is overwhelming. Sapphires are the next stones in the foundation and are the mineral corundum—. pinkish-red to red corundum stones, which are called rubies. They include all the other colors of corundum: blue, pink, green, yellow, violet, purple, orange, brown, white, gray, and black. Next, we see the Chalcedony, which can exhibit colors of pale lavender-blue to lavender-purple, pink, and white. The fourth stone mentioned in the foundations is the emerald, which is a green beryl. Emeralds typically display a deep green color, but can also be seen with yellowish or blueish tones. The fifth foundation stone was the sardonyx, which is a variety of onyx that usually contains flat-banded, white and brownish-red bands. Onyx is a gemstone with alternating light and dark bands , which are colored in brown, red, black, white, and grey. As I'm sure you can see the 'Light Show' these gems can put on is astonishing.

"Moving a little further down the line, we see the sixth foundation stone. This stone is called the sardius, it appears to be unknown in modern gemological circles. Some Bible scholars connect it with carnelian, which is a red-orange variety of agate. The seventh gem is chrysolite, which is a golden variety of the mineral peridot. Peridot can be olive green, green, yellow, or brown in color.

"Beryl is the next stone we view. The term beryl covers a number of different minerals, including aquamarine (blue to blue-green to sea-green), bixbite (red beryl), emerald (green beryl), goshenite (colorless beryl), heliodor (golden/yellow beryl) and morganite (pink beryl)."

We are all astounded at the incomparable beauty of the city. Truly, Jesus is the master builder. He has spent over 3,000 years constructing this home for His bride and there is nothing to compare it to.

"Keep in mind that each of these foundations has the name of one of the twelve apostles on it. What does this represent? Jesus told His church in Matthew 5:14: *'Ye are the light of the world. A city that is set on an hill cannot be hid.'* The church that Jesus established during His earthly ministry was commissioned to show the light— Christ to a lost and dying world. He let them know that they were not the light but that they were to reflect the Light of the World" John 8:12: **"***Then spake Jesus again unto them, saying, I am the light of the world: he that followeth me shall not walk in darkness, but shall have the light of life.***"** "This New Jerusalem that you see before you represents the relationship that Jesus has with His bride, (His church,), down through the ages. Each foundation carrying one of the apostles' names shows another dimension of the differing colors of light that are all being illuminated by Jesus Christ— the source of *all* light.

"Foundation number nine reveals a stone called topaz, it is "commonly colorless," but it also appears in a wide variety of colors, light to medium blue, yellow / orange / pink / red / violet with or without brown tone, brownish green, and brown. The tenth stone is the chrysoprase whose colors include, pale green, yellowish green, apple green, deep green. Jacinth is the eleventh stone, which is a variety of the mineral zircon. Jacinth occurs in the clear, transparent red, orange, and yellow colors. Finally, we look at the amethyst, which is a variety of quartz. Its colors are light to dark purple.

"We are going to be looking at the gates in the wall as we travel to our next stop. There is a total of twelve gates in the city, the first gate is 375 miles from where we are right now it is going to be about another four hours till we arrive. Just sit back and enjoy the ride and the beauty of this new heaven."

Seven

Day One - Evening

After traveling for many hours and being overwhelmed by the beauty of this AMAZING place, many questions have entered our minds. Our angel guide has been relatively quiet as we have made the journey on our way to the first gate. One of the first questions I am eager to ask when we stop will be: "What are these vast cities we have been passing on the right-hand side of the bus?" Since our journey began, we have traveled almost 375 miles and as far as our natural eyes can see, there are millions of happy people and large beautiful buildings that appear to be their homes. There are several streets with what looks like special activities happening in different areas. Some of the places look like parks with stunning landscapes, the people seem happy. If we were back on earth, as we know it, we might think we were at the entrance to a large city like Los Angeles.

The multitudes of people we see don't even seem to notice us as they busy themselves with projects—actually, we are not really sure what it is they are doing.

Suddenly, my thoughts are diverted by the loud sounds of *"Whew!"*

"Wow!" as the others in the bus start expressing sounds of excitement and awe at something that is coming into view ahead of us. We must be getting close to the first gate as there is an amazing light show coming out of the wall of the city. It's different from the combinations of light and colors we have seen up to now. Never in our wildest dreams did we think anything could get any more spectacular than what we had already seen but—we were wrong.

As our group gets closer to the gate, the scenery before us is breathtaking. I wish I had a better vocabulary to describe what we are seeing. It is the most majestic, astonishing, and remarkable scene I have ever witnessed. Remembering the many times the Bible instructed me to "fear" the Lord, I think I understand better what that reverence should have produced. What I am experiencing right now as I view this entrance to the city of God, humbles me. This is where I should always be when handling the Word of God or considering my relationship with Him.

So far, we have seen things which have exceeded our level of comprehension. In the past when I read 1 Corinthians, 2:9 *"But as it is written, Eye hath not seen, nor ear heard, neither have entered into the heart of man, the things which God hath prepared for them that love him."* I didn't know what that was talking about. My tour through heaven is beginning to open my eyes to how much God loves His children and the things He has planned for our future.

The bus has pulled to the edge of the road a few blocks from the gate and the entrance to the city. Our angelic tour guide has stood and now, all of our attention is on him. "It's time for another disclaimer," he says, as all of our attention has shifted to him. "You have probably noticed that the people you have seen on our journey thus far seem unaware of your presence. The reason for this is because all of you are in human form. As I mentioned when we first began this trip, the world is different now. The final fire of judgment cleansed the world of all elements of sin. Everything connected with the sin curse that came upon the world when Adam violated God's law in the Garden of Eden, has been removed. You have been allowed to take this tour by looking into the inspired Word of God. There are places we won't be able to go and again, there will be things I can't share with you. The purpose of this trip is for you to get a glimpse of the prize!" Philippians, 3:13-14 *"Brethren, I count not myself to have apprehended: but this one thing I do, forgetting those things which are behind, and reaching forth unto those things which are before, I press toward the mark for the prize of the high calling of God in Christ Jesus."* "Hopefully, all of the wonderment of what God has prepared for those who are "pressing" toward the mark will get our lives focused on LOVING and serving Him with all of our being."

Having given us this information, he pulled the bus right up in front of the gate. What we are viewing is a bit unnerving to everyone in the group. We are in uncharted territory, and I can see by the look on everyone's faces that they are disoriented and afraid of facing the unknown. The angel senses this as well, and he begins to calm us by assuring us that God is allowing us to view these things so that our understanding of His promises might become more relevant in the future. With his words of assurance, our fears are quelled. He continued: "We are getting ready to consider some things, which might seem like an unveiling of mysteries but, in fact, are based on clear scriptures.

"Some have asked me questions about the peoples and the activities we have seen on the right side of the bus. We began our trip at the southwest corner and have been traveling east all day. Our bus has traveled along the wall, which put the nations of the saved to our right side. Up until now, I have kept mostly quiet on the subject but there are some things we need to discuss before I begin to tell you about the entrance to the city and the beautiful gates you are viewing.

Let's examine Revelation, 21:23-27:

> *And the city had no need of the sun, neither of the moon, to shine in it: for the glory of God did lighten it, and the Lamb is the light thereof. And the nations of them which are saved shall walk in the light of it: and the kings of the earth do bring their glory and honour into it. And the gates of it shall not be shut at all by day: for there shall be no night there. And they shall bring the glory and honour of the nations into it. And there shall in no wise enter into it any thing that defileth, neither whatsoever worketh abomination, or maketh a lie: but*

40

they which are written in the Lamb's book of life.
(Revelation 21:23-27)

"The information revealed in these scriptures has often been passed over by Bible 'teachers' down through the ages. When scriptures are not considered in context, wrong conclusions are made. Where are these nations of saved people located? Who are they and why don't they live in the New Jerusalem?"

The angel looks at each of us intently and asks this simple question; "Where are we?" He gets several responses; "We are in heaven. We are in the new heaven and the new earth. We are at the New Jerusalem." When the answers have finished he asks another question. "Where are hell and the lake of fire?" Answers are not coming as quickly with this question, but there seems to be plenty of "I'm not sure" shrugs.

Our angel guide does not give us a direct answer, but at this point, he turns our attention to Revelation 20, which gives us much information about the chronology of the end times. The beginning of the chapter reveals that the seven years of tribulation have finished and God has bound Satan in a bottomless pit for a thousand years.

Revelation, 20:1-2: *"And I saw an angel come down from heaven, having the key of the bottomless pit and a great chain in his hand. And he laid hold on the dragon, that old serpent, which is the Devil, and Satan, and bound him a thousand years."*

"The next order of events is the thousand-year reign of the faithful "overcomers" with Christ on the 'old' earth. This began with the resurrection of all the children of God from Adam down to the last saved person. A blessing is pronounced on all who are part of the 'first' resurrection."

> And cast him into the bottomless pit, and shut him up, and set a seal upon him, that he should deceive the nations no more, till the thousand years should be fulfilled: and after that he must be loosed a little season. And I saw thrones, and they sat upon them, and judgment was given unto them: and I saw the souls of them that were beheaded for the witness of Jesus, and for the word of God, and which had not worshipped the beast, neither his image, neither had received his mark upon their foreheads, or in their hands; and they lived and reigned with Christ a thousand years. But the rest of the dead lived not again until the thousand years were finished. This is the first resurrection. Blessed and holy is he that hath part in the first resurrection: on such the second death hath no power, but they shall be priests of God and of Christ, and shall reign with him a thousand years. (Revelation 20:3-6)

Next, we are told that Satan will be released from the bottomless pit at the end of the thousand-year reign of Christ on the earth. He gathers a great army from the humans still living on the earth who refused to accept Jesus as Savior and King of the world. A battle takes place, called Gog and Magog and the number of lost people in Satan's army is huge. The end result of that battle is that God sends fire from heaven and completely devours all the lost. Finally, Satan is cast into the "lake of fire" where he will be tormented day and night for all eternity:

> *And when the thousand years are expired, Satan shall be loosed out of his prison, And shall go out to deceive the nations which are in the four quarters of the earth, Gog and Magog, to gather them together to battle: the number of whom is as the sand of the sea. And they went up on the breadth of the earth, and compassed the camp of the saints about, and the beloved city: and fire came down from God out of heaven, and devoured them. And the devil that deceived them was cast into the lake of fire and brimstone, where the beast and the false prophet are, and shall be tormented day and night for ever and ever. Revelation 20:7-10*

What happens next is the dread of all of God's children. All of our acquaintances who rejected Jesus as their Savior are going to be cast into the "lake of fire." Verses eleven through fifteen tell us that death and hell are delivered up and cast into the lake that burns with fire throughout all eternity. Every person from Adam's generation down to this final day of judgment who rejected Jesus (Messiah,) are forever separated from God:

> *And I saw a great white throne, and him that sat on it, from*

whose face the earth and the heaven fled away; and there was found no place for them. And I saw the dead, small and great, stand before God; and the books were opened: and another book was opened, which is the book of life: and the dead were judged out of those things which were written in the books, according to their works. And the sea gave up the dead which were in it; and death and hell delivered up the dead which were in them: and they were judged every man according to their works. And death and hell were cast into the lake of fire. This is the second death. And whosoever was not found written in the book of life was cast into the lake of fire. (Revelation 20:11-15)

"At this time there are only two types of humans left, the lost who are abiding in the lake of fire and the saved children of God who will live in the presence of God for all eternity.

"A fire has cleansed the earth of all evidence of sin and the curse is gone. The new heaven and the new earth have been placed on the earth." The angel looks at us again and says "Now tell me where are the lost?" The answer he receives this time is a resounding, "eternally separated from God!" He goes on to say, "It is not important for us to know where the lake of fire is—whether it is in the center of the earth, or in some other location that God has decided to put it. All that I wanted you to see is that all of these people, houses, and activities going on outside of the New Jerusalem have nothing to do with lost, unsaved people. There are no human bodies living on the outside of the city. They are all children of God in glorified resurrection bodies. Furthermore, though these living in the nations on the outside of the New Jerusalem did not qualify to be a part of the bride of Christ, they are not being punished— there are no tears in heaven!

"The last thing I need to explain to you before we look at the gate and entrance to the city, is the information found in Revelation, 21:24: *'And the nations of them which are saved shall walk in the light of it: and the kings of the earth do bring their glory and honour into it.'* Two things are discovered from this verse. The first is, nations of saved people live on the outside of the New Jerusalem. Not only do they live on the outside of the city but also they are not allowed to enter the new city."

The angel catches the shocked looks on some of the people in the tour group's faces and says: "I know, you have heard differently from some of your Bible commentators, but bear with me, we will see what the Bible says! The next thing we notice is the kings who are governing over these nations of saved people on the outside. They will be the ones able to go into the city and bring the praises, glory, and honor of their subjects before Jesus. Who these kings are and how they got their jobs will be considered later in the tour. Why aren't these nations of saved people able to go into the city? Again, we will examine that at a later point. But, for now, let's all take a deep breath because we are about to take a closer look at the gate and the entrance."

Eight
The Pearly Gate

It is doubtful that there is anyone reading this book who has not heard something in their lifetime about the pearly gates. Very likely, you may have heard about it in a joke where Saint Peter met someone at the "pearly gate" to determine whether they would be allowed into heaven. I have never heard one that even came close to any teaching of the Bible. Most of them were very doctrinally unsound, presenting some form of salvation by the performance of good works. You may have wondered where the idea of the pearly gates of heaven came from. The answer to that question will be seen as we take a closer look at the gates of the New Jerusalem.

Our angel guide has redirected our attention to the first gate on the southern wall of the New Jerusalem. He states, "Before us is one of twelve entrances to the holy city. There are three on each side of the city." We listen to his words but the depth of our ignorance is overwhelming. I ask myself, how could I have read the Bible verses that talk about this and never perceived the magnitude of what they were saying? The inadequacies of my vocabulary surprise me. I want to share with others how glorious this place is, but I can't find the words. How could I read God's inspired words describing this marvelous gate and entrance and only picture a plain door or opening in my mind's eye? I am struggling to find an expression that would describe what I am seeing.

 The words of our guide bring me back to a consciousness of where I am and what I am being allowed to see. He continues his observations by saying he wants to quote the scriptures that describe this place. Revelation, 21:3: *"And I heard a great voice out of heaven saying, Behold, the tabernacle of God is with men, and he will dwell with them, and they shall be his people, and God himself shall be with them, and be their God."* The angel states, "We are in the presence of God, this is where He lives." That revelation stuns me and everyone on the bus—I am in the presence of God? The almighty God? Jehovah? We are in the place where God lives?! The God who in six days created the universe and all that is in it. Tears fill our eyes Wow! Fear and reverence overwhelm us.

        The angel continues: "The apostle Paul tells us about going to the place where God dwelt, 2 Corinthians, 12:2: *'I knew a man in Christ above fourteen years ago, (whether in the body, I cannot tell; or whether out of the body, I cannot tell: God knoweth;) such an one caught up to the third heaven.'* That 'third' heaven has transferred to the new earth."

 He redirects our attention to the city entrance where we have stopped.

"Listen to what the Bible says about this location." Revelation, 21:12-13: "*And had a wall great and high, and had twelve gates, and at the gates twelve angels, and names written thereon, which are the names of the twelve tribes of the children of Israel: On the east three gates; on the north three gates; on the south three gates; and on the west three gates.*"

"We are sitting in front of the first gate on the south side of the city. It is 375 miles from the corner where we began our journey. The next gate will be 375 miles from here and the remainder of all of the gates will be spaced that same distance from each other. All of the gates will look similar to this one.

"Each gate will have an angel located at the entrance. You may have wondered why there is a great and high wall going around this city and angels sitting at the entrances to the city? Throughout the Old Testament, we find cities built with high fences and guards at the gates to scrutinize who could come into the cities. The walls were also there as protection against enemies who would come against the city. We know, here in the eternal heaven ages, there won't be any lost people and no sin present, so why are they here? Our first thoughts might be that they are symbolic. Something very important must be represented for twelve angels to have this job for eternity. It is not clear whether it will be the same angel at each gate or whether they will have other angels that will replace them at different times. One thing is clear, they do add to the beauty of the entrance."

There is some interesting information about the gates of this city; Revelation, 21:21: *"And the twelve gates were twelve pearls; every several gate was of one pearl: and the street of the city was pure gold, as it were transparent glass."*

We're again faced with the task of putting our minds into "'operational mode'" to comprehend what a pearl this size would look like. Everyone in this tour bus is mesmerized and again,we are struggling with our limited vocabularies. This pearl is so large, it is an entrance gate to the largest, most spectacular structure ever created. To see one so huge and know that there are eleven more like it at the other gates of the city is almost unimaginable. The largest natural pearl known to man is about ¾ of an inch in diameter. Our guess to the size of this gate would be something close to twenty feet in diameter. It is reported that the ¾ inch natural pearl would have taken many years to develop! How long would it take to make one the size of this gate? Seems like a good time to again consider; John, 14:2-3 *"In my Father's house are many mansions: if it were not so, I would have told you. I go to prepare a place for you. And if I go and prepare a place for you, I will come again, and receive you unto myself; that where I am, there ye may be also."* It has been over two thousand years since our Lord spoke these words. Even if Jesus were to return today, there would still be at least another thousand years for His earthly reign before the New Jerusalem will arrive. It is always interesting to listen to the scoffers say things like: "It would be impossible to make a natural pearl that size." These are the same ones who question whether God could make the universe and all that is in it in six literal 24-hour days!

Pearls are a very unusual kind of gem. One unique aspect about them is their iridescence. This means their surface color changes, based on the angle of the light hitting them. Because the light upon this pearl is coming from Jesus and His throne, it is different than the light produced by the sun. Not only is it the purest form of light coupled with the colors radiating from the foundation stones and the iridescence of the pearl, it's beauty is heavenly. John, 8:12 *"Then spake Jesus again unto them, saying, I am the light of the world: he that followeth me shall not walk in darkness, but shall have the light of life."* We should not wonder at the marvel of this eternal dwelling place of God and His special bride. James 1:17-18 *"Every good gift and every perfect gift is from above, and cometh down from the Father of lights, with whom is no variableness, neither shadow of turning. Of his own will begat he us with the word of truth, that we should be a kind of firstfruits of his creatures."*

Some have concluded that these pearly gates are just large doors that are coated with pearl. While this may be easier to get our mind's eye connected to, a literal understanding of what the Scriptures reveal seems to be a better choice. Isaiah, 55:8-9: *"For my thoughts are not your thoughts, neither are your ways my ways, saith the LORD. For as the heavens are higher than the earth, so are my ways higher than your ways, and my thoughts than your thoughts."*

Our angel guide has given us some time to just view and examine the scene before us. Knowing we have never witnessed anything like this, he gives us time to take it all in. He gets our attention by pointing to the opening that the pearl would cover if it was shut. The opening to the city is round and it is the exact size of the pearl. The frame that the pearl is hinged upon is made of pure gold, so finely polished that it is like a mirror. It seems so precision-made, like that of a bank vault. It appears evident that if the pearl door was closed the exactness of the fit would make it air-tight.

Of course, we know that it will not be closed. Nevertheless, its perfection is not lost on our senses. Revelation, 21:25 *"And the gates of it shall not be shut at all by day: for there shall be no night there."* Looking beyond this opening it is round like a tunnel, and it continues along the full width of the wall. The width at the base of the wall is 216 feet, and it appears as though this tunnel is about that same length long. At the end of this tunnel opening, the light is very bright. Just past the door opening, the tunnel structure widens and the height increases, but it keeps the tunnel-like appearance. The bottom is flat and is an extension of the gold street that is coming out of the city. The walls of this tunnel are pure gold. I have never seen gold polished like this. The Bible talks about God's words being purified; Psalms, 12:6: *"The words of the LORD are pure words: as silver tried in a furnace of earth, purified seven times."* The process of making gold and silver so pure that it would look like glass seems to be how this gold has been prepared.

The gold street proceeds out of the mouth of this opening for a short distance and then stops. One of the people in our group asks our guide a question.

"We have traveled, according to you, 375 miles to get to the entrance of the city. We have passed vast areas that appear to be like cities. We have seen many beautiful buildings and structures. There seems to be a vast amount multitudes of people. It appears that there are streets that travel throughout these areas and go for as far as the eye can see."

The angel interrupts and says, "I thought you had a question?"

"I'm getting to it," the questioner replies. "Why haven't we seen any gold streets before we got to the gate opening? I had always been taught that when we arrived in heaven all of the streets would be gold?"

The angel smiles and says, "Very observant."

"To answer your question," the angel replies, "We must look to the Bible for the answers." Revelation, 21:18 *"And the building of the wall of it was of jasper: and the city was pure gold, like unto clear glass."*

"We are also told in Revelation, 21:21: '*And the twelve gates were twelve pearls; every several gate was of one pearl: and the street of the city was pure gold, as it were transparent glass'."*

"Both of these scriptures have reference to the New Jerusalem that comes down from heaven to be placed on the new Earth. According to these verses, the gold streets and the walls of this new city appear to be gold. Everything you have been viewing up to this point has been on the outside of this special city that Jesus has prepared for His bride, (John, 14:2-3). What we have been viewing on our trip to the gate are the nations of the saved who live on the outside of the New Jerusalem. Revelation, 21:24-26: '*And the nations of them which are saved shall walk in the light of it: and the kings of the earth do bring their glory and honour into it. And the gates of it shall not be shut at all by day: for there shall be no night there. And they shall bring the glory and honour of the nations into it.*' I know this will open new questions for you and at some point, we will try to answer some of them."

Nine

We Three Kings

At Christmas time we sing the song,:

> "We three kings of Orient are,
>
> Bearing gifts, we traverse afar
>
> Field and fountain moor and mountain,
>
> Following yonder star" John H. Hopkins (1857)

Interestingly enough, the events of that visit may not be so different from what the kings over the nations of the saved in Revelation chapter twenty-one will be doing.

Matthew, 2:1 *"Now when Jesus was born in Bethlehem of Judaea in the days of Herod the king, behold, there came wise men from the east to Jerusalem,"* The Magi or Kings, came to Mary, Joseph, and Jesus after His birth to honor Him with gifts and acknowledge Him as the King of the Jews. Examining the information concerning the new heaven and new earth, we find a group of God's children who do not live in the New Jerusalem. They are described as "nations of the saved," and they have kings governing them and representing them. These kings are allowed to bring honor and glory from their subjects to the King of kings in the New Jerusalem. These nations are not allowed to go into the city personally but each nation has a king that who represents them. Those abiding in their nations want to offer up praises for the redemption they have received by the blood of the Lamb. This king is able to go before the throne of God and bring the praises of their subjects. The importance of their job becomes evident as we observe the things happening at and around the throne of God.

Revelation gives us information that no other book in the Bible reveals so clearly. The very name of the book says it all— "The Unveiling."

> *After this I looked, and, behold, a door was opened in heaven: and the first voice which I heard was as it were of a trumpet talking with me; which said, Come up hither, and I will shew thee things which must be hereafter. And immediately I was in the spirit: and, behold, a throne was set in heaven, and one sat on the throne. And he that sat was to look upon like a jasper and a sardine stone: and there was a rainbow round about the throne, in sight like unto an emerald. And round about the throne were four and twenty seats: and upon the seats I saw four and twenty elders sitting, clothed in white raiment; and they had on their heads crowns of gold. And out of the throne proceeded lightnings and thunderings and voices: and there were seven lamps of fire burning before the throne, which are the seven*

Spirits of God. And before the throne there was a sea of glass like unto crystal: and in the midst of the throne, and round about the throne, were four beasts full of eyes before and behind. And the first beast was like a lion, and the second beast like a calf, and the third beast had a face as a man, and the fourth beast was like a flying eagle. And the four beasts had each of them six wings about him; and they were full of eyes within: and they rest not day and night, saying, Holy, holy, holy, Lord God Almighty, which was, and is, and is to come. And when those beasts give glory and honour and thanks to him that sat on the throne, who liveth for ever and ever, The four and twenty elders fall down before him that sat on the throne, and worship him that liveth for ever and ever, and cast their crowns before the throne, saying, Thou art worthy, O Lord, to receive glory and honour and power: for thou hast created all things, and for thy pleasure they are and were created. (Revelation 4:1-11)

We can only see the things on the inside of the city by the information given to us in Revelation. Our angelic guide lets us know that our tour group cannot enter the city. We can only have access through the information God has given us in His inspired Word. Revelation chapters four and five lets us see things that humans had only been able to speculate about before these chapters were written.

The New Jerusalem has come down from heaven, Revelation, 21:2: *"And I John saw the holy city, new Jerusalem, coming down from God out of heaven, prepared as a bride adorned for her husband."* When the New Jerusalem arrived on the new earth, everything we discovered about heaven in chapter four was now on the new earth. Revelation, 21:1: *"And I saw a new heaven and a new earth: for the first heaven and the first earth were passed away; and there was no more sea."* The first heaven has passed away.

Most people who read chapter four and five in the Book of Revelation are pretty shocked to get a glimpse of the throne of God. Who knew before reading this that the illumination of God was like *"looking upon jasper and sardine stone?"* The jasper stone puts out a red or reddish brown color and sometimes yellow. The sardine stone is a blood red color. The rainbow around the throne is different from those we have witnessed on earth today, for it is radiating the colors of an emerald. I think this means its colors are the different shades of green seen in emeralds. We know from Moses' visit to Mount Sinai, when he received the Ten Commandments, that his face "shone" after being in the presence of God but until chapter four of Revelation, we did not know about the radiating color from God and the throne.

The 24 elders, the flying creatures, the thundering and lightning, all of this is new information. Probably, the most important piece of information is the constant direct praising and honoring of God that takes place. This information allows us to see how important these kings are in the worship process throughout eternity.

The New Jerusalem not only contains Christ and His bride but also, these things found in chapters four and five in Revelation. According to the information we acquire from Revelation, there are *astonishing* things going on in this special place prepared by Christ for His bride.

These kings, who are over the nations of the saved, have very important jobs. Revelation, 21:24-26: "*And the nations of them which are saved shall walk in the light of it: and the kings of the earth do bring their glory and honour into it. And the gates of it shall not be shut at all by day: for there shall be no night there. And they shall bring the glory and honour of the nations into it.*"

Two things stand out in these scriptures. First, there are nations of saved, born again believers who do not live in the New Jerusalem. They live in the light of the city, but they cannot go into it. Who are they and why must they live outside the New Jerusalem? We will try to find answers to these questions in future chapters. The second thing we notice is that these nations receive their light from the New Jerusalem. Revelation, 21:23: "*And the city had no need of the sun, neither of the moon, to shine in it: for the glory of God did lighten it, and the Lamb is the light thereof.*" Also in, Revelation, 22:5 "*And there shall be no night there; and they need no candle, neither light of the sun; for the Lord God giveth them light: and they shall reign for ever and ever.*" The heavens and new earth don't have the sun, moon, or stars to provide light. These sources are no longer needed, as Jesus has become the literal light of the whole world. In the world we live in today, Jesus is the spiritual light of the world. Mankind's only hope of escaping the darkness of sin is through belief in Jesus Christ as Savior. John, 8:12: *"Then spake Jesus again unto them, saying, I am the light of the world: he that followeth me shall not walk in darkness, but shall have the light of life."*

In the *eternal ages,* God's children will live on a new earth with a new heaven and there will be no need for external light. Just as in our present world the **sun** is the source of our light; on the new earth, the Son of God will be the source.

From the New Jerusalem, the light will pass through the outer edges of this 1500-mile cube, and its light will illuminate the whole earth. Each side of the city will shed light upon the nations that dwell on the outside. Remember, the city extends 1500 miles into outer space. The light will illuminate for thousands of miles on each side of the city. How far out from this city do the nations extend? We do not have any scriptures that answer this question. One thing we know— there will be no darkness in heaven and there will be no night.

We are told that there are nations. The Greek word for nations here is: *ethnos,* the root meaning is, tribe, race, or foreign. It depicts something more than a city. The nations are large and have kings who govern them. The idea of a place with large masses of people having no structure or government is not implied here. One of the jobs of these kings is to bring gifts of honor, love, and devotion from the saved they govern. These are children of God who love Jesus their Savior. They know that His love and grace have saved them from an eternity in the lake of fire.

The verses we have looked at so far have presented some information that may not line up with the things we have heard about heaven. The idea that everyone in heaven will be regarded in the same way does not line up with the scriptures we have considered. In the chapters ahead we will find even more evidence that God's judgment on the actions of His children's earthly lives is just.

In the account of the final judgment of all the saved, we gather some important information about how the eternal ages will be faced by God's born again children.

> *For other foundation can no man lay than that is laid, which is Jesus Christ. Now if any man build upon this foundation gold, silver, precious stones, wood, hay, stubble; Every man's work shall be made manifest: for the day shall declare it, because it shall be revealed by fire; and the fire shall try every man's work of what sort it is. If any man's work abide which he hath built thereupon, he shall receive a reward. If any man's work shall be burned, he shall suffer loss: but he himself shall be saved; yet so as by fire. (1 Corinthians 3:11-15)*

This is an examination of our life works from the time we accepted

God's free gift of eternal life through the sacrifice of His Son until the day we die. It is clear that not every saved person produces the same kind of lifestyle. This information should not shock any of us as we have personally witnessed the differences in how saved people have lived their lives. No one is born again into God's family by producing good works. Titus, 3:5: *"Not by works of righteousness which we have done, but according to his mercy he saved us, by the washing of regeneration, and renewing of the Holy Ghost."* We also know that we do not keep our relationship as God's children by doing good works. Isaiah, 64:6: *"But we are all as an unclean thing, and all our righteousnesses are as filthy rags; and we all do fade as a leaf; and our iniquities, like the wind, have taken us away."*

We know people who give testimonies of accepting Christ as their Savior and then walk in the flesh, committing many horrendous sins. I personally have known many who have lied, cheated, robbed, and were involved in adultery or fornication. Like King David who committed adultery and murder, we have witnessed these crimes by people who have professed Christ as their Savior. How many have divorced without having the scriptural grounds to do so? Even some who sexually abused children have claimed a faith in Christ. Some might conclude that all of these who do such things are not really saved. The reason we cannot accept this is because the Bible is continually showing us that saved children of God are still in fleshly sinful bodies. Saved people can do anything a lost person can do because we are still in the flesh.

The apostle Paul says it so clearly. I know this is a long set of verses but they answer the question of why saved people still sin:

> For other foundation can no man lay than that is laid, which is Jesus Christ. Now if any man build upon this foundation gold, silver, precious stones, wood, hay, stubble; Every man's work shall be made manifest: for the day shall declare it, because it shall be revealed by fire; and the fire shall try every man's work of what sort it is. If any man's work abide which he hath built thereupon, he shall receive a reward. If any man's work shall be burned, he shall suffer loss: but he himself shall be saved; yet so as by fire. (1 Corinthians 3:11-15)

> For we know that the law is spiritual: but I am carnal, sold under sin. For that which I do I allow not: for what I would, that do I not; but what I hate, that do I. If then I do that which I would not, I consent unto the law that it is good. Now then it is no more I that do it, but sin that dwelleth in me. For I know that in me (that is, in my flesh,) dwelleth no good thing: for to will is present with me; but how to perform that which is good I find not. For the good that I would I do not: but the evil which I would not, that I do. Now if I do that I would not, it is no more I that do it, but sin that dwelleth in me. I find then a law, that, when I would do good, evil

is present with me. For I delight in the law of God after the inward man: But I see another law in my members, warring against the law of my mind, and bringing me into captivity to the law of sin which is in my members. O wretched man that I am! who shall deliver me from the body of this death? I thank God through Jesus Christ our Lord. So then with the mind I myself serve the law of God; but with the flesh the law of sin.
(Romans 7:14-25)

The list could go on concerning saved people who have not honored God with their lives but on the other side, we see those who have loved the Lord with all their hearts. They love reading and studying God's Word. They pray daily for others and seek God's direction for their lives. Some are great soul winners, and many are faithful to God all of their lives. Where would His church be if it had not been for His children who walked in the Spirit and not followed the lust of the flesh?

The Scriptures, concerning the final judgment of God's children reveal important information. Not all the saved will be honored for righteous living in eternity. "Some will be saved, yet so as by fire." They make it to heaven but God is not able to say, "Well done good and faithful servant." Those who have lived exemplary lives, loving God with everything they have will be given some special attention. These faithful children will wear crowns that reveal their love and dedication to their Savior and espoused bridegroom. They will be distinguished from the unfaithful children who will not have this recognition of faithful service. The faithful bride will live with Jesus in the mansion He has prepared for them. They will eat fruit from the tree of life on the inside of the city. However, the unfaithful will not be allowed to eat the fruit from the tree of life, but they will get the leaves. We will talk more of this in future chapters.

The final evidence of what the "Judgment Seat of Christ" has produced will be seen in the new heaven. Some will live in the New Jerusalem and some will live in the nations of the saved on the outside of this great city. It may be possible that each nation will have different citizens based on the results of the judgment. If there were differences in the population of the nations, what would they be? Most likely, they would be based on the results of the final judgment.

We know all born again children of God will be in heavenly bodies, 1 John, 3:2: *"Beloved, now are we the sons of God, and it doth not yet appear what we shall be: but we know that, when he shall appear, we shall be like him; for we shall see him as he is."* So, it would not be an issue of appearance but one of the degrees of judgment. Perhaps the one "saved, yet so as by fire" would not be in the same nation with those who had produced works of righteousness, but had not met the qualifications to be a part of the bride of Christ? We will consider more about this matter in later chapters.

Who are the kings who rule over the nations? We again are left without concrete information on the identity of the kings. We could speculate and consider some possibilities. They might be kings chosen from the faithful of the Old Testament Israel. They could be very faithful Christian people who were not part of the bride because they were ignorant of the qualifications, but lived very righteous lives. They, no doubt, will be special servants chosen by God for a job that will be very challenging. While we might not figure out exactly who they are until we get there, it is clear their job is very important.

Ten
Puffy Clouds

Where are the clouds and the boring clothing of heaven? How often have you seen heaven pictured as a place where the children of God are wandering around heaven in puffy white clouds in plain robes, seemingly with no real purpose or destination? The Scriptures we have considered so far paint a much different picture— God is a colorful God! The examination of the walls of the city with all of their jewels of color and the translucent pearl gates that refract the light and the colors of the city make it clear that heaven will be a colorful place.

The dress of the priest of Israel was made of beautifully embroidered threads and colorful breastplates made of stunning gems set in gold. Exodus 28:4-6:

> And these are the garments which they shall make; a
> breastplate, and an ephod, and a robe, and a broidered
> coat, a mitre, and a girdle: and they shall make holy
> garments for Aaron thy brother, and his sons, that he
> may minister unto me in the priest's office. And they
> shall take gold, and blue, and purple, and scarlet, and
> fine linen. And they shall make the ephod of gold, of

*blue, and of purple, of scarlet, and fine twined linen,
with cunning work. (Exodus 28:4-6)*

The kings of Israel would also wear similar clothing on special occasions. What would make us think that it would be any different as God has concluded this age and begins the eternity of the new heaven? Most likely, when the kings over the nations of the saved come to bring the praises and honors of the nations they rule, they will be dressed in a similar manner. Like the kings who came to honor Jesus at His birth, it may be that the kings of the nations will come in groups of three. Three is a very prominent and significant number in the Bible, (i.e. Trinity, Jesus three days and nights in grave, etc.) A delegation of kings would seem appropriate. My mind's eye can imagine three kings marching to the city of God, dressed in garments that acknowledge the wonder and marvel of God. Making their way through the streets that connect the different nations. Shouts and sounds of praises would follow them as they march to the city entrance. Trying to get a feel for what it would be like, I imagine earthly parades like the Macy's Thanksgiving parade or the Rose Bowl parade. Multitudes line the streets; excitement is pulsing through the crowds as their king travels to the throne of God. God's blood-bought children are thrilled about their king delivering offerings to the King of kings!

The angel, who is placed at the pearl gate would acknowledge their arrival. Possibly, trumpets or musical instruments would announce their arrival. The worship of God around His throne is exciting to all of

His children. Those who live on the inside of the city are glad to see the kings from the nations arriving with their offerings. Nothing boring about heaven—all of the angels, all of the creatures, all of God's family, busy loving the great and mighty God of all creation.

Wow! Look at those bodies! In the world we live in today, it can be an amusing afternoon to go to your local mall, find a seat, and enjoy the show. It's not just the crazy way people dress when they go out in public that provides the entertainment. From the babies to the geriatric crowd the differences in how we present ourselves can be quite the performance. From mischievous little children running and hiding behind a bush to a teenager trying to look like the sophisticated adult. Then there is the octogenarian struggling with their walker to make it to the orthopedic shoe store. Many wonder what will we look like in heaven, 1 Corinthians 15:35,: *"But some man will say, How are the dead raised up? and with what body do they come?"*

Our minds shift into gear, and our reasoning process is engaged when we read, "With what body do they come?" Will little children's bodies be part of the heavenly population? Will some have senior bodies but in perfect working order? Some may reason that all of our bodies will be at the "perfect" age when they performed at their highest level of excellence, maybe 21-25-year old bodies. Have you ever heard a person of advanced years say they wished they could have their knowledge and experience in a younger body? Or looked at a group of children operating in hyper mode and made a statement like: "I wish I had their energy with my knowledge?" The question might be, "What is the *perfect* age?" I suppose the answer would depend on what we want to accomplish. If we want an Olympic gold medal, we would choose the young vibrant body. If we were struggling with a business decision, we would want the mind of a seasoned successful entrepreneur.

We struggle to imagine what it will be like in the eternal age. We battle with time and age in this life because it plays such an important role today. In the new heaven and new earth, time will be no more. After a billion years have passed, the eternal dweller will appear no older than when the new age began. What will our bodies look like? 1 John 3:2-3: "*Beloved, now are we the sons of God, and it doth not yet appear what we shall be: but we know that, when he shall appear, we shall be like him; for we shall see him as he is. And every man that hath this hope in him purifieth himself, even as he is pure.*" What a blessing to know that we will have a body like Jesus! Philippians 3:21: "*Who shall change our vile body, that it may be fashioned like unto his glorious body, according to the working whereby he is able even to subdue all things unto himself.*"

Everyone who lives in the new heavens will have spiritual bodies changed by God to be the bodies we live in forevermore:

> *Behold, I shew you a mystery; We shall not all sleep, but we shall all be changed, In a moment, in the twinkling of an eye, at the last trump: for the trumpet shall sound, and the*

dead shall be raised incorruptible, and we shall be changed. For this corruptible must put on incorruption, and this mortal must put on immortality. So when this corruptible shall have put on incorruption, and this mortal shall have put on immortality, then shall be brought to pass the saying that is written, Death is swallowed up in victory. O death, where is thy sting? O grave, where is thy victory? (1 Corinthians 15:51-55)

These are the bodies we all long for, bodies that are free of pain, active, and vibrant—and bodies that will never die.

Those who live in the New Jerusalem will have bodies just like the bodies of those who live in the nations of the saved. What is worn on their new bodies might be different. At the marriage of Jesus, His bride wears a special wedding garment that portrays her righteous living while in human bodies. Revelation 19:7-8: "*Let us be glad and rejoice, and give honour to him: for the marriage of the Lamb is come, and his wife hath made herself ready. And to her was granted that she should be arrayed in fine linen, clean and white: for the fine linen is the righteousness of saints.*"

The Bible also says to the faithful overcomers of Sardis in, Rev 3: "*He that overcometh, the same shall be clothed in white raiment...*" Again, we find special garments being offered to the children of God who overcame sin in their lives. The idea that saved people can live sinful and faithless lives and then find themselves in the eternal ages enjoying all of the blessings of those who loved and served their Savior doesn't fit what the Bible says.

We understand that we are not born into the family of God by doing good works. It is also understood that our salvation is not kept by doing good works. Titus 3:5: "*Not by works of righteousness which we have done, but according to his mercy he saved us, by the washing of regeneration, and renewing of the Holy Ghost.*" God securely keeps His children even when we have been disobedient to His commands. That doesn't mean His grace will reward disobedience. God has set many blessings, opportunities, and rewards before His righteous children. The evidence of God's rewards on those children who loved His Son with all of their beings will be clearly seen throughout eternity. God's approval of them will be obvious by the special garments, the crowns they wear, the location of their residences. Why will some of God's children wear crowns while others will not? Righteous living is a requirement—not an option for God's children. God offers the crowns with specific requirements on each for those who will receive them, (i.e. the martyr's crown requires the loss of physical life as a result of standing for God's truth.) For now, we conclude that loving Jesus in this life with all of our heart, mind, and soul will determine the circumstances of our living in the new heaven.

God is a righteous and just judge. Logical reasoning would indicate that a person who is born again and then lives contrary to the teachings of Jesus would not be rewarded for bad behavior. John 15:10, "*If ye keep my commandments, ye shall abide in my love; even as I have kept my Father's commandments, and abide in his love.* " All of the New Testament scriptures teach that we will be judged according to our works. 2 Corinthians 5:10, *"For we must all appear before the judgment seat of Christ; that every one may receive the things done in his body, according to that he hath done, whether it be good or bad.* " In the next chapter, we are going to talk about why righteous living is necessary for born again believers. It should become clear that it is not to stay saved but to reveal our love for our Savior.

Eleven

Our Sins Past, Present, and Future

God's grace is astounding and remarkable on levels, which excel human reasoning! What a concept— that God who created everything would take a personal interest in us. Why would He, when we have all sinned and come short of His glory? There is an eternal lake burning with fire waiting for us at the final judgment. Why? Because by nature we are sinners. We do not have within us the ability to please God. We see the total depravity of our human sin nature when we listen to the angry crowd who wants to hang Jesus on the cross crying out, *"His blood be on us, and on our children!"* Only God's love and grace could deliver us from what we deserve. When we recognize the offering of the blood shed by Jesus Christ for the deliverance from our sins, past, present, and future, we stand amazed at the depth of His love. *Romans, 6:23 "For the wages of sin is death; but the gift of God is eternal life through Jesus Christ our Lord."*

In view of what we have already discovered about the new heaven and new earth, it seems important to address this gift. Our sins were in the future when Jesus died and shed His blood for the remission of

74

sins. Jesus was not only dying for the sins of those who had not been born, His payment reached all the way back to Adam. The payment for sin was made in full for all, including the disobedient during the times of Noah and even to those who lived during Christ's time on earth, (His present.) Yes, even for those who cried out, *"His blood be on us, and on our children!"* The question comes to mind, "What about the sins we commit after we are saved?" Does Christ's offering on the cross cover our sins throughout our lifetime, (our future?) Some may say, "If my future and present sins are paid in full, why is it necessary for me to confess and repent of them?" Let's examine what the Bible says about the need for forgiveness of sin. When we understand the extent of God's offering for our sins, it will become clear what is required of us.

The first thing we discover about humans is that we are all totally depraved from birth. Romans 5:12, *"Wherefore, as by one man sin entered into the world, and death by sin; and so death passed upon all men, for that all have sinned:"* The Psalmist confirms this fact, Psalms 51:5, *"Behold, I was shapen in iniquity; and in sin did my mother conceive me."* When someone says there is a little good in everyone, the Bible quickly rejects this idea as **not** true. We cannot produce the righteousness required that will please God and make us acceptable to enter heaven. Isaiah 64:6, *"But we are all as an unclean thing, and all our righteousnesses are as filthy rags; and we all do fade as a leaf; and our iniquities, like the wind, have taken us away."* Our sins, like the wind, have taken us away; when death comes, hell would be our eternal destiny, were it not for God's grace.

1 John 4:9-10, *"In this was manifested the love of God toward us, because that God sent his only begotten Son into the world, that we might live through him. Herein is love, not that we loved God, but that he loved us, and sent his Son to be the propitiation for our sins."*

"Propitiation" is an interesting word, meaning the turning away of wrath by an offering or appeasement to a deity. By one man, (Adam,), we all stood condemned to an eternity in hell. *Romans, 5:12 "Wherefore, as by one man sin entered into the world, and death by sin; and so death passed upon all men, for that all have sinned:"* Christ paid our sin debt, which had sealed our condemnation to hell in full. There was no one else who could have paid it, He was the only sinless one who could do it. Acts 4:12, *"Neither is there salvation in any other: for there is none other name under heaven given among men, whereby we must be saved."*

When Christ died on the cross, the full payment for sin was made for all. When I was physically born, the sin nature already had me condemned to hell. The payment for my condemnation had already been made. Did that mean I was already guaranteed to go to heaven? Not according to the words of Jesus, John 3:3, *"Jesus answered and said unto him, Verily, verily, I say unto thee, Except a man be born again, he cannot see the kingdom of God."* Even though the blood of Christ has been paid in full for all mankind in every age, not all will be saved. Romans 10:9-10, *"That if thou shalt confess with thy mouth the Lord Jesus, and shalt believe in thine heart that God hath raised him from the dead, thou shalt be saved. For with the heart man believeth unto righteousness; and with the mouth confession is made unto salvation."* Confession and belief is a requirement to receive eternal life and complete forgiveness of sin.

 Once a person receives Jesus Christ as their Savior something happens. We stand justified in the sight of God. The blood of Christ covers our past sins and sin condition. We are a new creation; we have a new spiritual nature. 2 Corinthians 5:17, *"Therefore if any man be in Christ, he is a new creature: old things are passed away; behold, all things are become new."* Does this mean that we will not sin anymore? This is an easy question to answer because anyone who has been saved more than a day knows the answer is: "Of course we do!" Are we happy that we still sin, No! Romans 7:14-17, *"For we know that the law is spiritual: but I am carnal, sold under sin. For that which I do I allow not: for what I would, that do I not; but what I hate, that do I. If then I do that which I would not, I consent unto the law that it is good. Now then it is no more I that do it, but sin that dwelleth in me."* If the apostle Paul struggled with the issue of sinning, no wonder we do also. Did he give up? No,

> *But I see another law in my members, warring against the law of my mind, and bringing me into captivity to the law of sin which is in my members. O wretched man that I am!*

> *who shall deliver me from the body of this death? I*
> *thank God through Jesus Christ our Lord. So then with*
> *the mind I myself serve the law of God; but with the*
> *flesh the law of sin. (Romans 7:23-25)*

Do the Scriptures teach that after we are saved the blood of Christ has paid for our future sins? In other words, has He already paid in full for the sins we started committing from the first day of our salvation until the day we die and leave for heaven? The answer is—*Absolutely, paid in full!* Does this mean we do not have to confess our sins and repent of them to take advantage of the payment? No, it does not, just like the lost person must repent and confess their faith in the sacrifice made by Jesus for acquittal, so the saved person must confess and repent for the payment to be applied.

The teaching in the religious world that our sins after the new birth are paid for and it is not necessary to confess and repent of them is unbiblical. Because of this kind of teaching, many children of God lead disobedient lives believing that when they get to heaven everyone will be rewarded equally. Some will look at our view of the eternal ages and reject the idea that the new heavens will have children of God who do not live in the New Jerusalem. They will reject the idea that children living inside the city will be able to eat fruit from the tree of life and children outside will not be able to enjoy it. These ideas will mess with their beliefs that everyone in heaven will have the same thing. Their doctrines in this life have led them to believe that it did not matter if they made a complete sacrifice for the Savior. It is sad that often, our pre-conceived ideas will keep us from the blessings God has in store for those who love Him:

> *Wherefore gird up the loins of your mind, be sober, and hope to the end for the grace that is to be brought unto you at the revelation of Jesus Christ; As obedient children, not fashioning yourselves according to the former lusts in your ignorance: But as he which hath called you is holy, so be ye holy in all manner of conversation; Because it is written, Be ye holy; for I am holy. (1 Peter 1:13-16)*

Twelve
Taking Up Our Cross

Does God's Word teach the need for the sanctification of our lives? Matthew 16:24, *"Then said Jesus unto his disciples, If any man will come after me, let him deny himself, and take up his cross, and follow me."* The scriptures have enlightened us concerning the new heaven and the new earth. Clearly, there are intriguing elements that make us believe there will be distinctions between the inhabitants. We have many scriptures that make us believe God expects us to be conformed to the image of His Son in this life. The idea of denying ourselves and taking up the cross of Jesus presents a sanctified life of separation from the world.

Sometimes, when the idea of working and obeying commandments is presented, the religious world identifies it as "legalism." We must always guard against a service that is not motivated by love but. Jesus said, *"If ye love me, keep my commandments."* John 14:15. James made it clear that we do not work to be saved, but our works demonstrate our love for God. James 2:17-18, *"Even so faith, if it hath not works, is dead, being alone. Yea, a man may say, Thou hast faith, and I have works: shew me thy faith without thy works, and I will shew thee my faith by my works. "* The "high calling of God" demands a special life from those who will be a part of the bride of God's Son. The bride, that Jesus will marry, will be presented to Him without spot and blemish:

> *Husbands, love your wives, even as Christ also loved the church, and gave himself for it; That he might sanctify and cleanse it with the washing of water by the word, That he might present it to himself a glorious church, not having spot, or wrinkle, or any such thing; but that it should be holy and without blemish. Ephesians 5:25-27*

What does a church without spot and blemish look like? In the first book of Corinthians, there was a church member who was committing fornication. As a member of this church we would assume that he was saved, had baptism acceptable to God, and was part of the Lord's church in Corinth. The church was instructed to put him out of the membership. The reason given was that the "spirit" might be saved on the day of the Lord. This was not talking about the excluded man's spirit but the church's. The church will be presented at the marriage of the Lamb without spot and blemish. Very clear instructions are given about the church not tolerating members who choose to walk in sin:

> *But now I have written unto you not to keep company, if any man that is called a brother be a fornicator, or covetous, or an idolater, or a railer, or a drunkard, or an extortioner; with such an one no not to eat. For what*

have I to do to judge them also that are without? do

not ye judge them that are within? But them that are

without God judgeth. Therefore put away from among

yourselves that wicked person. (1 Corinthians 5:11-13

The instructions God leaves us in His Word concerning the

sanctification of His children's lives are very clear:

I beseech you therefore, brethren, by the mercies of God, that ye

present your bodies a living sacrifice, holy, acceptable

unto God, which is your reasonable service. And be not

conformed to this world: but be ye transformed by the

renewing of your mind, that ye may prove what is that

good, and acceptable, and perfect, will of God. For I

say, through the grace given unto me, to every man

that is among you, not to think of himself more highly

than he ought to think; but to think soberly, according

as God hath dealt to every man the measure of faith.

(Romans 12:1-3)

The idea of presenting our bodies as living sacrifices is such a graphic

statement that it should not leave any doubt as to God's expectation for

the bride of His Son! Not being conformed to this world makes it clear

that we cannot dress like, talk like, or act like the ungodly people we

live around in this world. Our commission from God is to go out and

preach the saving gospel of Jesus Christ to a lost and dying world but

not to become a part of it.

When Jesus asked for a lifetime commitment, many of His

disciples decided that this was too much to ask. Because they were unwilling to make a full pledge to Him they left Him and went back to their old selfish ways. John 6:53-54, *"Then Jesus said unto them, Verily, verily, I say unto you, Except ye eat the flesh of the Son of man, and drink his blood, ye have no life in you. Whoso eateth my flesh, and drinketh my blood, hath eternal life; and I will raise him up at the last day."* After hearing this they responded: *"Many therefore of his disciples, when they had heard this, said, This is an hard saying; who can hear it?"* John 6:60. He was asking much, but He knew it would benefit them in the eternal ages. In spite of this: *"From that time many of his disciples went back, and walked no more with him"* John 6:66. Paul by God's inspiration knew that giving up everything was worth the prize. This prize was being offered to the faithful men and women of God's church. Philippians 3:7-8, **"***But what things were gain to me, those I counted loss for Christ. Yea doubtless, and I count all things but loss for the excellency of the knowledge of Christ Jesus my Lord: for whom I have suffered the loss of all things, and do count them but dung, that I may win Christ."* He was setting his eyes on the **mark**—it was the ultimate prize. This is God's greatest offering to His children. Philippians 3:13-14, *"Brethren, I count not myself to have apprehended: but this one thing I do, forgetting those things which are behind, and reaching forth unto those things which are before, I press toward the mark for the prize of the high calling of God in Christ Jesus."* The **high calling** of God in Christ Jesus—to be married to His

Son and live in that special mansion He has prepared for His bride throughout all eternity. Wow! Paul understood that living for the things of this world was the equivalent of a pile of refuse. He knew that obedience to the teachings and commandments of God would produce great rewards beyond our imagination.

As a church planter, Paul understood his work was about separating the children of God into greater relationship with Christ. He knew that bringing saved children of God into the Body of Christ, (the church) was not to get them saved or to keep them saved. 2 Corinthians 11:2-3, *"For I am jealous over you with godly jealousy: for I have espoused you to one husband, that I may present you as a chaste virgin to Christ. But I fear, lest by any means, as the serpent beguiled Eve through his subtilty, so your minds should be corrupted from the simplicity that is in Christ."* The church in Corinth was engaged to be the bride of Christ, but some of the actions of her members were jeopardizing that relationship.

In the first letter to their church, they had excluded the man guilty of fornication. Now, this man has repented of his sin, returning to the church with a desire to serve the Lord. However, some people in the church don't want to accept his apology and restore him to the fellowship. The church realized that they could not allow its members to practice sin and be part of the body of Christ. Now, he has repented of his sin and wants to be a member again. But the prideful spirits of some are refusing him membership. The sin of pride is a terrible sin that can keep a church from loving Jesus as we are commanded to do. 1 John 2:16, *"For all that is in the world, the lust of the flesh, and the lust of the eyes, and the pride of life, is not of the Father, but is of the world."* Keeping the church of Jesus without spot or wrinkle is a full-time job. Mostly, it is a job in which each member must be involved, keeping our own pride and fleshly sin under control. Titus 2:12-14, *"Teaching us that, denying ungodliness and worldly lusts, we should live soberly, righteously, and godly, in this present world; Looking for that blessed hope, and the glorious appearing of the great God and our Saviour Jesus Christ; Who gave himself for us, that he might redeem us from all iniquity, and purify unto himself a peculiar people, zealous of good works."*

The more we examine God's teaching about Christian living, the clearer it becomes that not everyone will hear "Well done, good and faithful servant," from the Lord when we enter the eternal ages. The issue is not whether we will make it to heaven. Be clear on this issue, there is no question that every born again believer will spend their eternity in heaven. The issue is whether we have loved Jesus with all of our heart, soul, and mind.

Romans 8, considers the issue of the inheritance of God's faithful and unfaithful children:

> *And if Christ be in you, the body is dead because of sin; but the Spirit is life because of righteousness. But if the Spirit of him that raised up Jesus from the dead dwell in you, he*

that raised up Christ from the dead shall also quicken your mortal bodies by his Spirit that dwelleth in you. Therefore, brethren, we are debtors, not to the flesh, to live after the flesh. For if ye live after the flesh, ye shall die: but if ye through the Spirit do mortify the deeds of the body, ye shall live. (Romans 8:10-13)

Keep in mind that He is talking to born again, baptized, members of the body of Christ—the church in Rome. The context of the scriptures is not talking about saved people losing their salvation. He speaks of the indwelling spirit that enters every child of God the day we were are birthed into God's family.

Why do these scriptures present us as debtors? Salvation is free; it is the gift of God. It is not by works that we have done. Doing good works did not save us and God does not require us to do acts of righteousness to stay saved. Titus 3:5-6, "*Not by works of righteousness which we have done, but according to his mercy he saved us, by the washing of regeneration, and renewing of the Holy Ghost; Which he shed on us abundantly through Jesus Christ our Savior;*" God saved us because He loved us when we were not loveable. He wants us to serve Him because we love Him, and we want Him to be pleased with us. "*For we are his workmanship, created in Christ Jesus unto good works, which God hath before ordained that we should walk in them*" (Ephesians 2:1). Remembering who we were before we became the children of God ought to be the motivation for loving Jesus enough to serve Him. Ephesians 2:13, *"But now in Christ Jesus ye who sometimes were far off are made nigh by the blood of Christ."*

So often in the realm of Christendom, it is taught that because all of our sins have been forgiven, even our future sins, indicating that there is no need for daily sanctification of our lives is not necessary. But God expects us as His children to pick up our cross and follow Jesus. To do this, we must continually be approaching the throne of God to have our daily sins cleansed. *1 John, 1:9-10: "If we confess our sins, he is faithful and just to forgive us our sins, and to cleanse us from all unrighteousness. If we say that we have not sinned, we make him a liar, and his word is not in us."* Paul, inspired by God, taught the members of the church at Corinth that laboring was required. *"For we are labourers together with God: ye are God's husbandry, ye are God's building. According to the grace of God which is given unto me, as a wise masterbuilder, I have laid the foundation, and another buildeth thereon. But let every man take heed how he buildeth thereupon."* (1 Corinthians, 3:9-10). Picking up our cross and following our Savior is done because we love Him, and we love the relationship we have with Him as His espoused bride.

Thirteen

Sin Judged

Does God judge the sins of His children in this age and in the eternal ages? *Hebrews 9:27, "And as it is appointed unto men once to die, but after this the judgment:"* This truth doesn't only apply to those who die without Christ as their Savior. The born again children of God will also have to stand before God and give an account of their lives.

There are two major judgments revealed in the Bible. Both of them reveal that our life works will be judged. Let's look at the judgment of the lost in, *Revelation 20:11-15:*

And I saw a great white throne, and him that sat on it, from whose face the earth and the heaven fled away; and there was found no place for them. And I saw the dead, small and great, stand before God; and the books were opened: and another book was opened, which is the book of life: and the dead were judged out of those things which were written in the books, according to their works. And the sea gave up the dead which were in it; and death and hell delivered up the dead which

were in them: and they were judged every man
according to their works. And death and hell were cast
into the lake of fire. This is the second death. And
whosoever was not found written in the book of life
was cast into the lake of fire.

These verses reveal to us that all men, women, and young people who did not accept God's free gift of eternal life end up in this lake of fire that produces different degrees of eternal punishment. An examination of each person's life by the books (the Bible) will expose each one's life. How they lived will determine the degree of punishment given to them in the lake of fire. It is very possible that people who committed horrendous sins, i.e., child molesters, serial killers, persecutors of God's children, and those who heard the gospel but rejected it will receive greater punishment.

Possibly some people will be cast into the lake of fire who never heard the gospel. They may have been really good people by our worlds standards but if they haven't prayed to Jesus acknowledging that they know their sin caused Him to be crucified and ask Him to save them they are lost. It doesn't matter how good one might be, without Jesus, the lake of fire is their eternal destiny. *Acts 4:12, "Neither is there salvation in any other: for there is none other name under heaven given among men, whereby we must be saved."* The final nail in the coffin will be when each person is shown that his or her name is NOT in the Lamb's book of life.

The horror of this judgment ought to touch the heart of every saved person. It is our duty to present the gospel to the entire world. More specifically we are commanded to share God's plan of salvation to everyone we meet:

> *Son of man, I have made thee a watchman unto the house of Israel: therefore hear the word at my mouth, and give them warning from me. When I say unto the wicked, Thou shalt surely die; and thou givest him not warning, nor speakest to warn the wicked from his wicked way, to save his life; the same wicked man shall die in his iniquity; but his blood will I require at thine hand. (Ezekiel 3:17-18)*

This verse reveals that God is going to judge us for how we have shared the gospel. Will God's children be judged for how we have conducted our lives?

> *For we must all appear before the judgment seat of Christ; that every one may receive the things done in his body, according to that he hath done, whether it be good or bad. Knowing therefore the terror of the Lord, we persuade men; but we are made manifest unto God; and I trust also are made manifest in your consciences. (2 Corinthians 5:10-11)*

This Scripture says, we will be judged for everything we have done — good or bad. These verses are being given to the members of the church of Corinth. The warning is to the saved, baptized members of

one of God's churches. God expects us to carry out the Great
Commission:

> And Jesus came and spake unto them, saying, All power is given
> unto me in heaven and in earth. Go ye therefore, and
> teach all nations, baptizing them in the name of the
> Father, and of the Son, and of the Holy Ghost: Teaching
> them to observe all things whatsoever I have
> commanded you: and, lo, I am with you alway, *even*
> unto the end of the world. Amen. (Matthew 28:18-20)

The other judgment exposed in God's Word is found in 1
Corinthians chapter 3. This is the judgment of God's blood bought-
children, it is called the "judgment seat of Christ" mentioned in *2
Corinthians, 5:10-11 "For we must all appear before the judgment
seat of Christ; that every one may receive the things done in his body,
according to that he hath done, whether it be good or bad. Knowing
therefore the terror of the Lord, we persuade men; but we are made
manifest unto God; and I trust also are made manifest in your
consciences. "* The judgment here is not to determine whether we are
saved—, that was settled the day we received Jesus Christ as our
Savior. His payment to save us from our condemnation to hell was
complete.

Sometimes, this judgment is referred to as the "bema seat of
Christ." *Bema* is simply the Greek word meaning "place of judgment."
I have often seen where this judgment is called *bema* to indicate that

it's something other than a judgment for sin. A statement like this will be made; "We should not look at the judgment seat of Christ as God judging our sins, but rather as God rewarding us for our lives." It is true that rewards will be determined at this time, but it is also true that we will be judged for our sins! God is serious about His judgment of the sins of His children. We are wrong when we indicate to the saved that we can sin and not worry about being judged for it!

For other foundation can no man lay than that is laid, which is Jesus Christ. Now if any man build upon this foundation gold, silver, precious stones, wood, hay, stubble; Every man's work shall be made manifest: for the day shall declare it, because it shall be revealed by fire; and the fire shall try every man's work of what sort it is. If any man's work abide which he hath built thereupon, he shall receive a reward. If any man's work shall be burned, he shall suffer loss: but he himself shall be saved; yet so as by fire. (1 Corinthians 3:11-15)

The reason a saved person will *suffer loss* is because sins not repented of and uncommitted lives are judged. God will not reward lazy children whose lives did not demonstrated a love for Jesus.

Does God judge His children? In Acts 5, a man by the name of Ananias, with his wife Sapphira sold a piece of property and gave money to the church saying it was the full price they received for the land. They both lied, they had sold it for more and kept back part of it. Peter told them they had not lied to the church but to God. God caused

92

both to die immediately for their sin. Most of the time we do not get an immediate judgment for our sin. Because of grace we have an opportunity to repent and be fully exonerated. In 1 Corinthians 11, church members were corrupting the Lord's Supper and God said because of that, He was causing many to become weak and sickly and many were dying. All of these people mentioned were saved church members. We don't live our Christian lives with a fear that God might kill us at any time if we sin, but we should not live ignorantly believing that we will not be judged for sins, which we do not confess and ask God's forgiveness. *Matthew 12:36-37, "But I say unto you, That every idle word that men shall speak, they shall give account thereof in the day of judgment. For by thy words thou shalt be justified, and by thy words thou shalt be condemned."*

God expects us to be holy if we want to be part of the bride who is described as having no spot or wrinkle:

> *Wherefore gird up the loins of your mind, be sober, and hope to the end for the grace that is to be brought unto you at the revelation of Jesus Christ; As obedient children, not fashioning yourselves according to the former lusts in your ignorance: But as he which hath called you is holy, so be ye holy in all manner of conversation; Because it is written, Be ye holy; for I am holy. And if ye call on the Father, who without respect of persons judgeth according to every man's work, pass the time of your sojourning here in fear: (1 Peter 1:13-17)*

God expects us to be holy if we want to be part of the bride who is described without spot or wrinkle. The judgment seat of Christ won't be a family reunion, social event, or an enjoyable encounter for disobedient believers. It will be a JUDGMENT with Jesus Christ sitting in the Judge's seat. The Bible is clear—not all Christians will enjoy the same station and have the same honor and responsibility in heaven. Everyone who trusts in Christ has the same salvation and will go to heaven. But some will be rewarded for their Christian service, and everyone will give an account for their unrepentant sins. As a Christian, never think that we can get away with worldliness, sin, disobedience, or being careless about soul winning.

The Christian life demands separation from the world. Being engaged to Jesus with the hope of being married to Him throughout eternity ought to be the great motivator to keep us on track. We need to make sure our priorities are set by Bible principles. It is easy to get caught up in our own selfish interest and not put Jesus at the center of our lives. It is also easy to put our energy and interest in the things of this world. This world is going to pass away and then, we will face eternity. We have settled where we will spend eternity by receiving God's gift of salvation but how we will spend it depends on our being holy as He is holy! *Galatians 6:7, "Be not deceived; God is not mocked: for whatsoever a man soweth, that shall he also reap."*

Fourteen

Overcomers?

We're back in our tour bus journeying towards the next gate, which is 375 miles away from the last one. Everything we are seeing on the right side of the bus has our minds pondering these nations. We have noticed that the streets we are seeing are not made of asphalt or concrete, but they are not gold either. Many of us had always thought that all the streets of heaven would be made of gold. When we ask our angel guide about this, we are informed that the gold streets are only on the inside of New Jerusalem. The streets are still pretty impressive even though we are not sure what they are made from. We also see homes on the streets; I would describe them as mansions or at least very upper class in their design. It is clear to all of us that what we are seeing is far superior to anything we have on earth as we know it today. One of the travelers asks the angel, "Who lives inside the city?" His response is, "The overcomers live in there." Seems like a pretty short answer but when he is questioned further, he says, "You will have to examine the scriptures in Revelation 2 and 3."

It seems clear, he is not going to give us any more information so we decide to check the Bible out. We find a scripture that talks about overcoming Satan and his devices. 1 John 2:14, *"I have written unto you, fathers, because ye have known him that is from the beginning. I have written unto you, young men, because ye are strong, and the word of God abideth in you, and ye have overcome the wicked one."* This makes us think being an overcomer involves filling ourselves with God's Word so we can overcome the Devil when we are tempted to sin. We also found a scripture that revealed that our power to overcome sin is because the Holy Spirit indwells all of God's born again children. 1 John 4:4, *"Ye are of God, little children, and have overcome them: because greater is he that is in you, than he that is in the world."* We are starting to get the idea that being an overcomer has something to do with sanctified living.

The word **"overcomer"** is translated from the Greek *nikao* and its root meaning is to subdue, (literally or figuratively.) Its general use means to conquer, overcome, prevail, or get the victory. It's about having success or victory. We are made to think about the apostle Paul's description of how he lived his Christian life:

> *Yea doubtless, and I count all things but loss for the excellency of the knowledge of Christ Jesus my Lord: for whom I have suffered the loss of all things, and do count them but dung, that I may win Christ, And be found in him, not having mine own righteousness, which is of the law, but that which is through the faith of Christ, the*

righteousness which is of God by faith: That I may know him, and the power of his resurrection, and the fellowship of his sufferings, being made conformable unto his death; If by any means I might attain unto the resurrection of the dead. (Philippians 3:8-11)

Here he talks about the righteousness that comes through his faith in Christ. Our righteousness that we try to muster from our own abilities is like filthy rags. The righteousness that comes from our faith in Christ is produced by the power of the Holy Spirit and only comes to those who walk in the Spirit. Galatians 5:16, *"This I say then, Walk in the Spirit, and ye shall not fulfill the lust of the flesh."*

Overcoming deals with the total surrender to the One we love. We surrender to Jesus, so we might have victory over life. It would show a surrender of our resources, i.e. money, energy, families, and mind. There would be a surrender of our time; i.e. study, soul winning, helping widows and orphans, caring for the homeless and hungry. Furthermore, it would involve surrendering earthly connections, like Moms, Dads, siblings, best friends, jobs, beliefs other than God's Word. Luke 14:26-27, *"If any man come to me, and hate not his father, and mother, and wife, and children, and brethren, and sisters, yea, and his own life also, he cannot be my disciple. And whosoever doth not bear his cross, and come after me, cannot be my disciple."* In other words, these things can't be our number one priorities. This doesn't mean we wouldn't still love our family and friends. We would still have employment and activities other than those at the church but serving Jesus would always take precedence. John 6:60, *"Many therefore of his disciples, when they had heard this, said, This is an hard saying; who can hear it?"*

The information about *overcomers* is emphatically stated as Jesus addresses the seven churches of Asia in chapters 2 and 3 of Revelation. Let's examine what He says to each church and the significance as related to the New Jerusalem.

The first address is, *"Unto the angel of the church of Ephesus write..."* Jesus then speaks to this church about her performance. As we have concluded previously, God has expectations from His children that have set their lives apart in His church. He praises them for the hard work they have done and how they doctrinally have been faithful to His truths. Next, He told them He has some things against them. What a shock this must have been. Remember, John was writing down the exact words of Jesus, and he was to deliver this letter to the church in Ephesus. He was writing this while in prison on the Isle of Patmos. When he was released from his incarceration, he traveled to each of these seven churches and delivered the whole book of Revelation. Can you imagine the shock we would feel if a letter from Jesus Christ arrived at our church evaluating how we were performing? After telling us the things He was pleased with, He then pointed out the things that were disappointing Him. Wow! What a shocker!

"Nevertheless I have somewhat against thee, because thou hast left

thy first love." Revelation 2:4. They had stopped loving Jesus like they did when they were first engaged to Him. No doubt, they were like us when we get so caught up in doing our religious service that we lose sight of our love. Our motivation in service is not about us following the rules or making sure we don't anger God. We are motivated by our love for Jesus. We want to go to church and worship Him. We love singing the songs that reveal how much He loves us and letting Him know how much we love Him. We desire to read God's Word because it talks about the one we will marry. We love sharing the gospel because it lets us reveal how wonderful our Savior and future husband is. We, like young engaged couples here in this life, can't spend enough time with, or talk with others enough about the amazing man or woman we are engaged to. The Ephesus church needed to get their minds and hearts set in the right direction.

"Remember therefore from whence thou art fallen, and repent, and do the first works; or else I will come unto thee quickly, and will remove thy candlestick out of his place, except thou repent." Revelation 2:5. Falling away from our "first love" is serious business. This church was in jeopardy of losing her "candlestick" (Holy Spirit.) This is not talking about any of the saved members of this church losing the indwelling of the Holy Spirit. On the day of Pentecost, the church that Jesus established during His personal ministry here on earth, was indwelt with the power of the Holy Spirit. All true churches have the Holy Spirit in a special way. This church was in peril of

losing their identity with Christ as His future bride. Repentance was necessary.

This portion of scripture was being addressed to the church at Ephesus. Six more churches will be spoken to. All seven represent "true churches" throughout all ages. It will be clear with each address that the message is to the churches. The admonitions concerning *overcomers* are clearly to the churches, not all the saved. Revelation 2:7, *"He that hath an ear, let him hear what the Spirit saith unto the churches; To him that overcometh will I give to eat of the tree of life, which is in the midst of the paradise of God."* These promises are to the obedient ones who were baptized and added unto one of the Lord's churches.

What is the promise and what does it have to do with the New Jerusalem and the dwellers of that city? There is an amazing tree that we first heard about in the Garden of Eden. *Genesis 3:22, "And the LORD God said, Behold, the man is become as one of us, to know good and evil: and now, lest he put forth his hand, and take also of the tree of life, and eat, and live for ever:"* The fruit from this tree gives life—when it was in the Garden of Eden this is all we knew about it. We get new information in Revelation as we find the final resting place of this tree. Revelation 22:2, *"In the midst of the street of it, and on either side of the river, was there the tree of life, which bare twelve manner of fruits, and yielded her fruit every month: and the leaves of the tree were for the healing of the nations."*

There are a few new things revealed in this scripture. The first is that its location is on the inside of the New Jerusalem. Only *overcomers* will live where this tree is and will have the privilege to eat its fruit. The next new thing we learn is that it produces 12 different kinds of fruit. It is not totally clear to me if the twelve fruits are on it each month or whether it produces one fruit each month. Thus, a different fruit every thirty days. We usually don't think about time in the eternal ages but maybe, this is to help us understand with our human reasoning. The final new thing we learn is, there are leaves on this tree that are used for the healing of the nations. The only nations around at this time are the *nations of the saved* on the outside of the city. Then we find that the Ephesus church is promised a place in the New Jerusalem where they will be able to enjoy the fruit of the *tree of life*.

Jesus next says, "*And unto the angel of the church in Smyrna write; These things saith the first and the last, which was dead, and is alive*" Revelation 2:8. Again, He praised this church for the good she had been doing:

> I know thy works, and tribulation, and poverty, (but thou art rich) and I know the blasphemy of them which say they are Jews, and are not, but are the synagogue of Satan. (Revelation 2:9)

The first thing He lets them know is that He has a martyr's crown for those who die standing for His truths. We will discuss the crowns in another chapter.

A very unusual promise is made to the *overcomers* in verse 11, *"He that hath an ear, let him hear what the Spirit saith unto the churches; He that overcometh shall not be hurt of the second death."* Jesus told the church of Smyrna to listen to what the Spirit of God is promising to the churches. *Overcomers* will not be "hurt of the second death." The second death is talking about the lost being cast into the lake of fire forevermore. Revelation 20:14, *"And death and hell were cast into the lake of fire. This is the second death."* The members of these churches were all saved, baptized, set apart believers. How could a saved person be hurt of the second death? The apostle Paul said he wasn't going to be judged for not preaching the gospel to the lost. Acts 20:26-27, *"Wherefore I take you to record this day, that I am pure from the blood of all men. For I have not shunned to declare unto you all the counsel of God."* Paul was a soul winner and God expects all of His church to be witnessing to the lost who will suffer the *second death* if they don't repent and believe on Jesus. The unfaithful servant in 1 Corinthians the third chapter suffered loss, yet, he was saved. I believe this promise to the *overcomers* is that they will live in the New Jerusalem because, like Paul, they were pure from the blood of all men.

We have five more churches to consider, but we will look at them in the next chapter.

Fifteen
Persistence

When I was first saved, a pastor told me to avoid the book of Revelation. His reasoning was—because I was a young Christian it could be confusing and discourage me from reading my Bible regularly. It perhaps was good advice for one who had just been born again but his advice lingered on for several years with me being fearful to read it.

The meaning of the name Revelation comes from a Greek word *apocalypse*, and it means "uncovering" or "disclosure." It uncovers matters that had been hidden and discloses events that would happen long after it was written. The very name of the book ought to grab the curious mind of a believer in Christ. It's the last book of the "owner's manual," the Bible. This book, like the first book, Genesis, is dictated by God. Moses penned Genesis, but he was not present when God was creating the universe and all that is in it. Only God could describe the exact manner of how the world came into existence. John, in the last book, is again approached by Jesus and given information into the future that only God could reveal. The beauty of Revelation is the new information it provides. Many of the scriptures are not really new information, but new clarity is given to things already revealed in other scriptures.

The evidence given about the advantages of being *overcomers* gives much clarity to verses that talked about the sanctification of life. It presents the value of separating ourselves in Christian service. It reveals the advantages of being obedient to God's commandments. Also, it makes it clear that there will be heavenly losses to God's children who don't love Him with all their hearts and minds.

With this in mind, we are thankful for the truth revealed to us in this great book. We left our last chapter considering the church at Smyrna and the rewards promised her for being faithful unto death. Now, we will examine three more churches of the seven churches of Asia.

"And to the angel of the church in Pergamos write; These things saith he which hath the sharp sword with two edges." (Revelation 2:12). It is interesting to examine His introduction to this church at Pergamos: *"Saith he which hath the sharp sword with two edges."* Jesus assured this church that He knew they were serving Him in a place where "Satan's seat" is. There were even some in this church who taught heretical doctrines. He reassured His people that He is the mighty God and conqueror. It is also interesting to note how the Bible is described in Hebrews 4:12, *"For the word of God is quick, and powerful, and sharper than any twoedged sword, piercing even to the dividing asunder of soul and spirit, and of the joints and marrow, and is a*

discerner of the thoughts and intents of the heart." Our wars against Satan and forces of evil are not fought with knives and guns but with the **powerful word** of the almighty God.

Jesus acknowledged the evils that had a place in this church in Pergamos. The doctrine of Balaam and the doctrine of the Nicolaitans are two teachings that God hates. The doctrine of Balaam was the promoting of falsehood for financial reasons. The doctrine of the Nicolaitans has to do with leaders in the church controlling or dictating over the people. In God's church there must be an equality of each member. Having a person or group in a church that controls or rules over the other members of the body is a teaching that Jesus hates. He told the church to repent or He would intervene. We live in a world where churches often tolerate sin in their membership. They didn't practice the kind of discipline that the Corinthian church was commanded to do in chapter five. Often, it is because we don't want to offend anyone or it is a family member who is guilty. These scriptures need to remind us that our fear should not be that we would offend a member but that we would offend God.

After He addressed the problems of this church, He encouraged them concerning the promises to the overcomers. Revelation 2:17, *"He that hath an ear, let him hear what the Spirit saith unto the churches; To him that overcometh will I give to eat of the hidden manna, and will give him a white stone, and in the stone a new name written, which no man knoweth saving he that receiveth it."* Manna was a food God provided for Israel when they were in the wilderness. More than a million of God's people were preserved by this food. Exodus, 16, tells the story of how God provided. We are also told that a pot of the manna was placed in the Ark of the Covenant as a reminder of God's care and protection. Where is the Ark today and where will it be in the eternal ages? The Ark was placed in the temple in the Holy of Holies during the Old Testament worship of Israel. We are told that the temple of God will be in the New Jerusalem in the eternal ages. This promise to the overcomers is a promise of eternal preservation in that beautiful city where the overcomers live.

A message for Thyatira—; Revelation 2:18, *"And unto the angel of the church in Thyatira write; These things saith the Son of God, who hath his eyes like unto a flame of fire, and his feet are like fine brass."* Our attention is again captured by this description of our Savior. None of us question that Jesus is the very definition of love! But something different is being displayed here;; "eyes like unto a flame of fire," and "feet like fine brass" give us a look at the message bearer in a new light. The eyes examined the works of this church; He was in the seat of judgment. This should remind us of the judgment seat of Christ described in 1 Corinthians 3 where works are being tried by fire. **"Brass"** is the word for bronze or something that is brazen such as the brazen altar or the brazen laver used in the Old Testament— and it always indicates judgment.

Why is Jesus judging the brothers and sisters of this body of Christ?

"Notwithstanding I have a few things against thee, because thou sufferest that woman Jezebel, which calleth herself a prophetess, to teach and to seduce my servants to commit fornication, and to eat things sacrificed unto idols." (Revelation 2:20). Some of the church allowed false doctrine to be taught and tolerated some sins that would destroy them. 1 Corinthians 5:6-7, *"Your glorying is not good. Know ye not that a little leaven leaveneth the whole lump? Purge out therefore the old leaven, that ye may be a new lump, as ye are unleavened. For even Christ our passover is sacrificed for us:"* We again see that Jesus is **not** going to tolerate unrighteous living in the church that will be presented without spot and blemish as His bride. The promise to those who overcome is great, but it is not offered to the unfaithful children of God who disobey His commandments. Revelation 2:26-29: *"And he that overcometh, and keepeth my works unto the end, to him will I give power over the nations: And he shall rule them with a rod of iron; as the vessels of a potter shall they be broken to shivers: even as I received of my Father. And I will give him the morning star. He that hath an ear, let him hear what the Spirit saith unto the churches."* God is offering the privilege to the bride of His Son, to be a part of His eternal government. As stated in a previous chapter, the children of God will not walk around in clouds without purpose or direction. Those who receive "power over the nations" will have an opportunity to serve the Triune God who will govern all from His throne in the midst of the New Jerusalem. Does this mean that

kings over the *nations of the saved* will come from the bride? Or does it mean they will have authority over the kings who rule over the nations? We can only speculate, some of these things, we probably will not know for sure until we get there. The word "power" comes from the Greek word *exousia* and means authority.

What does this promise of being given the morning star mean? Revelation 2:28-29, *"And I will give him the morning star. He that hath an ear, let him hear what the Spirit saith unto the churches."* Jesus identifies Himself as the "Morning Star" in Revelation 22:16, *"I Jesus have sent mine angel to testify unto you these things in the churches. I am the root and the offspring of David, and the bright and morning star."* The faithful bride will be presented to Jesus Christ as His wife and she will be given the "Morning Star" to live with throughout eternity. The nineteenth chapter says she has made herself ready, and she is arrayed in white, which represents her righteous living while on earth. These scriptures ought to make all born again children seek righteousness in our lives that we might be part of the overcomers.

The next church in the list of the overcomers is Sardis. *"And unto the angel of the church in Sardis write; These things saith he that hath the seven Spirits of God, and the seven stars; I know thy works, that thou hast a name that thou livest, and art dead."* (Revelation 3:1). Who is addressing them? "He that hath the seven Spirits of God." This does not indicate that there are seven Holy Spirits. The number seven is the number of perfection or completeness. Isaiah 11:2, talks about seven aspects of the Holy Spirit. (1) Spirit of the LORD, (2) Spirit of wisdom, (3) Spirit of understanding, (4) Spirit of counsel, (5) Spirit of power, (6) Spirit of knowledge, (7) Spirit of the fear of the Lord. This is probably what He is referencing. What do the seven stars represent? Revelation 1:20, *"The mystery of the seven stars which thou sawest in my right hand, and the seven golden candlesticks. The seven stars are the angels of the seven churches: and the seven candlesticks which thou sawest are the seven churches."* This reference is to the close relationship He has with each of His churches. As we have already concluded, the number seven embodies completeness and perfection. The seven churches that Jesus writes the book of Revelation to symbolizes all true churches throughout history. John is instructed to write the words that Jesus gives him and then when released from prison to deliver the full book of Revelation to each of the churches. Revelation 1:11, *"Saying, I am Alpha and Omega, the first and the last: and, What thou seest, write in a book, and send it unto the seven churches which are in Asia; unto Ephesus, and unto Smyrna, and unto Pergamos, and unto Thyatira, and unto Sardis, and unto Philadelphia, and unto Laodicea."* This book became the final book of the Bible. It was passed on to other churches and finally was included in the final canons of the scriptures.

Jesus told this church, "I have not found thy works perfect." It appears that the Sardis church had become lax in holding up some of the doctrines of the Lord. He admonished them to repent that they might remain a true church. There are times when we are tempted as true churches, to let down our standards on some of the commandments of the Lord. We are approached by people who want to join our churches and told that if we would loosen up on our doctrines they would be willing to join us. Sardis is the example to us that God would not be pleased with us if we did so.

To this church, Jesus says there are some who have resisted these changes, they are overcomers. He has a huge promise for those who stand fast:

> *Thou hast a few names even in Sardis which have not defiled their garments; and they shall walk with me in white: for they are worthy. He that overcometh, the same shall be clothed in white raiment; and I will not blot out his name out of the book of life, but I will confess his name before my Father, and before his angels. He that hath an ear, let him hear what the Spirit saith unto the churches. (Revelation 3:4-6)*

Why is being clothed in white raiment such a big thing? I have mentioned the wedding garment in previous chapters but now, let's look at its relationship to living in the New Jerusalem. Revelation 19:7-8, *"Let us be glad and rejoice, and give honour to him: for the marriage of the Lamb is come, and his wife hath made herself ready. And to her was granted that she should be arrayed in fine linen, clean and white: for the fine linen is the righteousness of saints.*" This wedding garment is made out of the righteousness of the saints; it is spectacular to look upon. The description of Christ's garment at the transfiguration is described in, Mark 9:3, "*And his raiment became shining, exceeding white as snow; so as no fuller on earth can white them.*" This garment, made up of righteous works, shines because God is pleased with it. It's not the righteousness we try to muster in human flesh but that which comes from faith. Philippians 3:9, "*And be found in him, not having mine own righteousness, which is of the law, but that which is through the faith of Christ, the righteousness which is of God by faith:*"

This white marriage garment grants entrance and dwelling in the New Jerusalem:

> And one of the elders answered, saying unto me, What are these which are arrayed in white robes? and whence came they? And I said unto him, Sir, thou knowest. And he said to me, These are they which came out of great tribulation, and have washed their robes, and made them white in the blood of the Lamb. Therefore are they before the throne of God, and serve him day and night in his temple: and he that sitteth on the throne shall dwell among them. (Revelation 7:13-15)

In these verses, it talks of the martyrs who have died standing for God's truths. The white robe and access to the throne of God will not just be for the martyrs, but all those that have loved His appearing. 2 Timothy 4:8, "*Henceforth there is laid up for me a crown of righteousness, which the Lord, the righteous judge, shall give me at that day: and not to me only, but unto all them also that love his appearing*" (2 Timothy 4:8).

What about the promise to the *overcomers* at Sardis? "*I will not blot out his name out of the book of life, but I will confess his name before my Father, and before his angels.*" Can the birth of one, into God's family, be annulled? Is this verse indicating that one's name can be removed from the book of the saved? When we read Revelation 20:15, "*And whosoever was not found written in the book of life was cast into the lake of fire*" our first impression is that the book of life contains all the names of the born again children of God. Those whose names are not in it will be cast into the lake of fire at the final judgment of the lost. I would conclude that all saved people are in the book of life. From the statement to the *overcomers*, the context would indicate that there is a section in this book where the names of those who will be in the bride of Christ are listed. If a person departs from a commitment to Christ, his or her name is removed. It may even be possible that this is a separate book. Whether there are two different books or a section of the book, which distinguishes the *overcomers*, I am not sure. The one thing I am sure of is that God's Word doesn't contradict itself! We have two more churches to consider among the seven churches and they both have something unusual about them. For this reason, I am going to include them in the next chapter.

Sixteen

Joint Heirs with Christ

"To have and to hold from this day forward, for better, for worse, for richer, for poorer, in sickness and in health, to love and to cherish, until we are parted by death. This is my solemn vow." These are the formal words for our earthly marriages. They convey that we will do whatever is necessary to be together throughout our entire earthly life until death separates us. The great thing about the marriage of Jesus Christ to His church in the eternal ages is that there is no death. The commitment to the vows has already been sealed before we leave this world.

> *And if children, then heirs; heirs of God, and joint-heirs with Christ; if so be that we suffer with him, that we may be also glorified together. For I reckon that the sufferings of this present time are not worthy to be compared with the glory which shall be revealed in us. For the earnest expectation of the creature waiteth for the manifestation of the sons of God. (Romans 8:17-19)*

Every born again child of God is going to be an heir of God. Titus 3:5-6, "*Not by works of righteousness which we have done, but according to his mercy he saved us, by the washing of regeneration, and renewing of the Holy Ghost; Which he shed on us abundantly through Jesus Christ our Saviour; "* Salvation is a free gift, which cost us absolutely nothing. Several things happen the very moment we repent and believe on the Lord Jesus Christ. The Holy Spirit of God indwells us immediately at the birth. Instantly, full access to God through prayer is granted. We are assured that nothing can separate us from His love; not even our own disobedience to Him. Resurrection bodies are guaranteed to everyone who is saved when Christ returns. At no cost, all of these things happen the moment we receive Christ as Savior.

 Romans, chapter 8, reveals something more: if we are children of God, we are heirs of God. This too was acquired the day we were born into God's family. Besides being "heirs," it also says we have the opportunity to become "joint heirs." *"And joint-heirs with Christ; if so be that we suffer with him, that we may be also glorified together."* Suffering with Christ involves something more than repenting and receiving the free gift of eternal life. Philippians 1:29, *"For unto you it is given in the behalf of Christ, not only to believe on him, but also to suffer for his sake."* What is the difference between an *"heir"* and a *"joint heir"*?

 Romans 8:17-19 definitely makes a distinction between an heir and a joint heir by inserting the conjunction **"if."** This little word puts a condition on being a joint heir and something is required to receive this position. An heir is someone who receives an allotted possession by right of sonship. The term "joint heir" is a legal one meaning a "'co-heir'," most often associated with married couples. By right of marriage, the two share equally in all possessions. Christ's bride will share in the mansion He has prepared for her, (New Jerusalem). She will also share in all of the eternal activities that Christ will execute. It will be worth it to be an overcomer.

The promises Jesus made to the *seven churches of Asia* are about His church suffering for Him. Historically, looking at the faithful church martyrs reminds us of how much suffering has happened to those who took the opportunity to be a part of the bride of Christ and suffering for Him seriously. I said in the last chapter that we would save our consideration of the final two churches because of some things that made them a little different. Let's look at them now.

The church of Philadelphia is the church that is **not** rebuked for corrupt works. Out of the seven, she is the only one that is fully commended for her faithfulness to Jesus. Revelation 3:7, "*And to the angel of the church in Philadelphia write; These things saith he that is holy, he that is true, he that hath the key of David, he that openeth, and no man shutteth; and shutteth, and no man openeth.*" Even the name of this church, (Philadelphia – brotherly love) signifies a group that exemplifies the love of God.

Christ presents Himself as the One who can open doors and shut them when necessary. It appears that Philadelphia loved soul winning; they loved the Great Commission and God opened doors for them. Matthew 28:19-20, *"Go ye therefore, and teach all nations, baptizing them in the name of the Father, and of the Son, and of the Holy Ghost: Teaching them to observe all things whatsoever I have commanded you: and, lo, I am with you alway, even unto the end of the world. Amen."* Most likely, the greatest threat to our churches today in remaining the true churches of God is a lack of commitment to these instructions of Jesus. His introduction to this church reminds us that we serve a God who can open doors. Our ministries do not have to be limited because we serve the great door opener. It is also good to know He will let us know when the door has been shut. Luke 9:5, *"And whosoever will not receive you, when ye go out of that city, shake off the very dust from your feet for a testimony against them."*

The overcomer rewards for Philadelphia are interesting:

> *Behold, I come quickly: hold that fast which thou hast, that no man take thy crown. Him that overcometh will I make a pillar in the temple of my God, and he shall go no more out: and I will write upon him the name of my God, and the name of the city of my God, which is new Jerusalem, which cometh down out of heaven from my God: and I will write upon him my new name. He that hath an ear, let him hear what the Spirit saith unto the churches. (Revelation 3:11-13)*

Philadelphia is told that she can become a "pillar" in the

temple of God. When I think of pillars, I see a big colonial plantation home with large columns that go up the front of the building supporting an upper deck. Truthfully, being a pillar doesn't sound very exciting. The term "being a pillar in the temple of God" is a metaphor, and now, it is probably a good time for us to consider the use of metaphors.

The dictionary definition is: A metaphor is a figure of speech in which an implied comparison is made between two different things that actually have something important in common. The word *metaphor* itself is a metaphor, coming from a Greek word meaning to "transfer" or "carry across." Metaphors "carry" meaning from one word, image, or idea to another. (http://grammar.about.com/od/qaaboutrhetoric/f/faqmetaphor07.htm) Mark Fenison does a wonderful job discussing the metaphor in his book, *"The Bride of Christ."* He talks about the metaphorical use of the church as the "body of Christ." He discusses the metaphorical presentation of the church as a "bride" and the "head" of the church being Christ. He considers the "espousal" metaphor concerning Christ and the church. I highly recommend reading his book.

How does the comparison made between a faithful church and pillar reveal important things they have in common? This metaphor is also used in, 1 Timothy 3:15, *"But if I tarry long, that thou mayest know how thou oughtest to behave thyself in the house of God, which is the church of the living God, the pillar and ground of the truth."* Here, the

118

doctrines and truths preached and taught by the true churches are compared to a "pillar" and to solid ground. In a world confused and frustrated with the events of life, the church stands as a solid reliable place for answers to the question, "What is truth?" The lighthouse metaphor presents the same idea as the pillar of truth. Matthew 5:14, *"Ye are the light of the world. A city that is set on an hill cannot be hid."*

Let's examine the promise made to the overcomers of Philadelphia. *"Him that overcometh will I make a pillar in the temple of my God,"* Where is this temple? *"And I saw no temple therein: for the Lord God Almighty and the Lamb are the temple of it."* In the New Jerusalem God Almighty and the Lamb, (Christ), are the temple. The throne of God is the seat of government. The pillar is a support and God is offering Philadelphia a seat in the government over everything throughout the eternal ages. It further says, they will *"go no more out."* When we looked at the throne of God in heaven described in chapter four in Revelation, we saw 24 seats that elders sat upon. They were clothed in white and had gold crowns on their heads. And out of the throne proceeded lightnings, thunderings, and voices: and *there were* seven lamps of fire burning before the throne, which are the seven Spirits of God. There were four beasts, (creatures) that day and night cry out "Holy, Holy, Holy, Lord God Almighty." If in our mind's eye, we can get a glimpse of the glory of those who had a part in that worship and exalting of God, we might better understand the magnitude of this promise to Philadelphia.

Three more marvelous things are promised to these faithful servants. *"And I will write upon him the name of my God, and the name of the city of my God, which is new Jerusalem, which cometh down out of heaven from my God: and I will write upon him my new name."* This promise is about the identity of the bride. Revelation 21:2, *"And I John saw the holy city, new Jerusalem, coming down from God out of heaven, prepared as a bride adorned for her husband."* The name of God, the name of God's city, and the name of Christ is the ultimate "prize." The city, New Jerusalem is called the bride. The name of God represents His blessing on the marriage of His Son. Finally, the name of Christ will be given to His bride. The pinnacle of every marriage is when all of the vows have been said, rings exchanged, candles lit, and the minister presents to the witnesses the newly married couple. He says I present to you, "Mr. & Mrs. _____. The congregation is not shocked that the bride had entered the marriage with one name and at the conclusion of the marriage ceremony, she has a new name.

The Philadelphian church was highly exalted because she had suffered with Jesus and stood firm in His truths. She was a soul-winning church and a church that exhibited the love of God.

We have finally come to the last of the churches that represented the true churches of Jesus Christ. I don't believe these churches represent dispensational ages. I believe all of these churches represent churches in every age. The trials, tribulations, blessings, and commitments can be seen in any church in any age. Their examples are not given to us to examine other churches and judge them as Philadelphian churches or Laodicean churches. All true churches ought to be examining themselves to see if any of the good or bad qualities of these churches exist in them. I said in my previous chapter that I had saved these last two churches because of their differences. As we have seen, the Philadelphia church was not rebuked for poor performance. We will see something very different in the final church.

Revelation 3:14, "*And unto the angel of the church of the Laodiceans write; These things saith the Amen, the faithful and true witness, the beginning of the creation of God.*" The final "Amen," speaks. All of His authority is based on ownership, "*the beginning of the creation of God.*" In other words, "I created it all, I am the only authority."

Jesus is **not** very happy with this church in Laodicea. Sometimes, when we are very displeased with something, we find a word or a thought to make it absolutely clear how upset we are. Jesus does something similar here when He tells this church they have made Him sick enough to vomit. Revelation 3:15-16, "*I know thy works, that thou art neither cold nor hot: I would thou wert cold or hot. So then because thou art lukewarm, and neither cold nor hot, I will spue thee out of my mouth.*"

What has made Him so upset? Revelation 3:17, "*Because thou sayest, I am rich, and increased with goods, and have need of nothing; and knowest not that thou art wretched, and miserable, and poor, and blind, and naked.*" Here is a church walking in the flesh. They are without faith in God, they think they can do it on their own. Hebrews 11:6, "*But without faith it is impossible to please him: for he that cometh to God must believe that he is, and that he is a rewarder of them that diligently seek him.*" The issues of this church, above all the others, ought to get our attention. It is easy to get caught up in religious activity without looking to God for strength and direction. If we don't start our days with a prayer, asking God to keep us humble, deliver us from evil, and give us wisdom in all decisions—we have started our day wrong. Strong Christians, admit to God that we are weak and have need of everything. For example, when decisions made in the church are based on whether the bank account can provide the ability to accomplish the goal, we have lost sight of "Who" controls everything.

Listen to the counsel of Jesus as He recommends to this church and all true churches throughout the ages, where our hearts should be fixed. Revelation 3:18, "*I counsel thee to buy of me gold tried in the fire, that thou mayest be rich; and white raiment, that thou mayest be clothed, and that the shame of thy nakedness do not appear; and anoint thine eyes with eyesalve, that thou mayest see.*" The gold that He counsels us to buy is righteousness. 2 Corinthians 5:21, "*For he hath made him to be sin for us, who knew no sin; that we might be made the righteousness of God in him.*" Our righteousness will always be rooted in Jesus and must be accomplished through faith.

Finally, as upset as Christ was with the Laodicean church, He still encourages them with a promise to those who overcome. Revelation 3:21-22, *"To him that overcometh will I grant to sit with me in my throne, even as I also overcame, and am set down with my Father in his throne. He that hath an ear, let him hear what the Spirit saith unto the churches."* Only the bride will sit with the King of kings! Truly this is the "High Calling of God in Christ Jesus."

As with all of the other seven churches, the admonition is: *"He that hath an ear, let him hear what the Spirit saith unto the churches."* As much as some would like to teach that sanctification of life after one is saved is not necessary, the Bible will not support that position. Being saved, baptized, and then surrendered to a local, visible church that practices everything the Bible teaches is a prerequisite.

Jesus is engaged to the bride (His church). Contrary to the teachings of many, **not** all the saved are going to be a part of the bride. If He is only engaged to His church and not to a universal body made up of all believers, it would seem important to be faithful in one of His churches. We have considered the overcomers for three chapters, and it has been clear that the promises made are not for everyone. We have also looked at the scriptures revealing what the new heaven and new earth will look like. It seems clear from scripture that there are nations of saved people who live on the outside of the New Jerusalem. If everyone will be the same, and have the same things in the eternal ages, why are there different locations for God's children? As we continue to look at the Scriptures for answers to these questions, we will be able to keep an open mind until all the evidence is presented.

Seventeen
What's It Like?

We have been traveling for several days now and have covered more than a thousand miles. We remain mesmerized at the sights we have seen. When Jesus said in John 14 that there were many mansions in His Father's house, most of us on this tour never comprehended the staggering numbers that would include. I suppose most of us were so focused on the mansion Jesus was promising to build for His bride that we didn't give much attention to the other mansions. As we have toured the new heaven, we have viewed mansions for as far as the eyes can see in all directions. Another surprising element which has never occurred to me is that they are all different. Even though they have similar characteristics, each one is distinctive in appearance. When I had read about nations of saved people it had not occurred to me that these children of God would not be living in the New Jerusalem.

Throughout our journey, our "angel guide" has been asked many questions about what it is like on the inside of the "special" mansion Jesus prepared for His bride. We were told at the first gate we viewed that we were forbidden to enter. We were privileged to see the entourage of the kings who were bringing the glory and honor of their nations into it. We were all so excited watching the procession with the people shouting and praising them along their journey to the gates of the city. We wanted to jump out of our bus and follow them in to get a glimpse of the ceremony on the inside. NO! We were emphatically informed that no unclean thing could enter this holy city. We were shocked! We said that we are saved children of God, our sins have been washed by the blood of the Lamb of God. The angel informed us that we were still in human bodies, and they could not enter the city.

One of the passengers asked why the saved on the outside of the city couldn't go in. He reasoned that they were born again believers who had their sins cleansed by Jesus, and they were in new glorified bodies. The angel reminded us about the trial by fire that had taken place at the judgment seat of Christ. All blood-washed children of God made it to heaven—but some suffered loss. He told us we would have to search the Scriptures for ourselves to discover why disobedient, unrepentant children, would not be allowed in the city.

Because all of us on the tour were still in human form, we continued to pester the angel about what the inside of the city looked like. He encouraged us to "Read Revelation, it's full of answers! Go back to Revelation chapter four and five. You need to get your finite minds thinking big. Remember, the total interior structure is 3,375,000,000 cubic miles. Think about where the throne of God is located. Do you think it would be located in the middle of the bottom of this great structure? If you expanded your horizons could it possibly be in the middle of the whole structure, which would make it 750 miles up to the center of it?

"When you have read these two chapters, in what kind of space do you picture all these things happening? Have you pictured something that would take place in a space like a football stadium? How much space would it take to house the amount of angels described in Revelation 5:11, *'And I beheld, and I heard the voice of many angels round about the throne and the beasts and the elders: and the number of them was ten thousand times ten thousand, and thousands of thousands.'* This may not be a literal number but one meaning innumerable. The numbers described here would be over 200,000,000. The heavenly description here in Revelation is about what the 'third heaven' is like right now. All of this will be moved to the inside of the New Jerusalem." Widening our concepts seems like a good suggestion from our guide.

Another person from our group asked for more information concerning the "tree of life." The first time we hear anything about this tree it is found in the Garden of Eden. *Genesis 2:9, "And out of the ground made the LORD God to grow every tree that is pleasant to the sight, and good for food; the tree of life also in the midst of the garden, and the tree of knowledge of good and evil."* It appears that all of the trees in the garden were good for food, even the tree of the knowledge of good and evil. It is not well defined whether Adam and Eve had eaten from the fruit of this "tree of life," but it is clear that after sinning, they were blocked from eating from it again. Once cast out of the garden, cherubims were placed at the gate to keep them from the tree of life:

> *And the LORD God said, Behold, the man is become as one of us, to know good and evil: and now, lest he put forth his hand, and take also of the tree of life, and eat, and live for ever: Therefore the LORD God sent him forth from the garden of Eden, to till the ground from whence he was taken. So he drove out the man; and he placed at the east of the garden of Eden Cherubims, and a flaming sword which turned every way, to keep the way of the tree of life. (Genesis 3:22-24)*

The tree of life on the inside of the New Jerusalem is presented to us in *Revelation 22:2, "In the midst of the street of it, and on either side of the river, was there the tree of life, which bare twelve manner of fruits, and yielded her fruit every month: and the leaves of the tree were for the healing of the nations."* There is also a very interesting set of Scriptures in the Old Testament that sounds very similar. *Ezekiel 47:12:*

> *And by the river upon the bank thereof, on this side and on that side, shall grow all trees for meat, whose leaf shall not fade, neither shall the fruit thereof be consumed: it shall bring forth new fruit according to his months, because their waters they issued out of the sanctuary:*

and the fruit thereof shall be for meat, and the leaf

thereof for medicine.

These Scriptures may be giving Israel information about their future opportunities. Abraham served God with the hope of a special city made by God:

By faith Abraham, when he was called to go out into a place

which he should after receive for an inheritance,

obeyed; and he went out, not knowing whither he

went. By faith he sojourned in the land of promise, as in

a strange country, dwelling in tabernacles with Isaac

and Jacob, the heirs with him of the same promise: For

he looked for a city which hath foundations, whose

builder and maker is God. (Hebrews 11:8-10)

The "overcomers" from the church of Ephesus were promised that as a reward, they would be able to eat the fruit from the tree of life. *Revelation 2:7, "He that hath an ear, let him hear what the Spirit saith unto the churches; To him that overcometh will I give to eat of the tree of life, which is in the midst of the paradise of God."*

The tree of life described in Revelation 22 produces twelve different kinds of fruit. Nothing is said in Genesis about the tree producing more than one kind of fruit. That, of course, doesn't mean that it didn't. Before Adam and Eve disobeyed God and ate the forbidden fruit, they were eternal in their human form and, therefore, it would not have been a problem for them to eat eternal fruit. Once they sinned, God put them out of the garden so they could no longer eat of the fruit, which would have made them live eternally in sinful bodies.

Revelation 22:2 states that there is more than one tree. There are trees on each side of the river. In the garden, there were only two people to eat from it. In the New Jerusalem, there are likely millions who will eat from it. We do not know exactly how many will live in the city but we have some clues given concerning who the bride will be. *Revelation 2:10, "Fear none of those things which thou shalt suffer: behold, the devil shall cast some of you into prison, that ye may be tried; and ye shall have tribulation ten days: be thou faithful unto death, and I will give thee a crown of life."* Here, a crown for the martyrs who have died standing for the truths of God is offered to the overcomers. The history of the Lord's true churches reveals massive numbers who gave their lives during the "dark ages." It would seem that at least this group would be part of the bride that lives in the city.

Startling information is given concerning this tree of life. Its leaves are used for the healing of the nations. Our ears perk up when we hear about healing in the eternal ages because there isn't supposed to be any sickness. What do we do with this information? We can't throw this Scripture out, we must investigate the meaning. Where are we going to find nations at this time? The millennial reign has ended. The judgment of the lost is completed and all who were judged were cast into the lake of fire. We are not sure where the lake of fire is located, but it is not even close to the new heaven and new earth. This tree of life and its contents are for the children of God who are living eternally with God. Those who live on the inside of the city have free access to the fruit. Those who live on the outside of the city cannot come into the city and eat the fruit.

The only nations that we have any information about are described as the "nations of the saved." They live on the outside of the city and can only have their kings enter into it. The conclusion has to be that these leaves are for those nations. What kind of healing do they need? Physical sickness is not the only kind of ailment that needs healing. We are not given specific information about this healing, but it may have something to do with God comforting those who are not able to live in the city. The kinds of medicines that are made from leaves are often ointments made for muscle discomfort. Possibly, there will be mental discomfort from realizing they could have lived in the New Jerusalem and eaten fruit from the trees had they loved Jesus more while they lived in their earthly bodies. We struggle with the idea of a need for healing because of what is said in *Revelation, 21:4 "And God shall wipe away all tears from their eyes; and there shall be no more death, neither sorrow, nor crying, neither shall there be any more pain: for the former things are passed away."* God never contradicts Himself and it is clear that He says that the leaves off of the tree of life on the inside of the New Jerusalem will be used for healing the nations of the saved. From what we have already learned these nations are those living on the outside of the New Jerusalem. Why there is a need for healing we can only speculate. Possibly the context of Revelation 21:4 makes that application to only those who live on the inside of the city.

It is hard, with our finite minds, to comprehend the glory and splendor of this place Jesus has prepared for His bride. Isaiah 55:9, probably says it the best; *"For as the heavens are higher than the earth, so are my ways higher than your ways, and my thoughts than your thoughts."*

There is a river that runs through the city. *Revelation 22:1, "And he shewed me a pure river of water of life, clear as crystal, proceeding out of the throne of God and of the Lamb."* We are again overwhelmed with thoughts concerning this river. What does it look like proceeding out of the throne of God and the Lamb? Because it seems possible that the throne of God is up in the middle of the city, would it be like a Niagara Falls coming out of the throne? Could it be like a Yosemite Falls or a Victoria Falls? As it flows through the city for hundreds of miles— will it be calm and flowing softly or will it be fast and powerful? If it flows to give the water of life freely to even those on the outside of the city—will it flow in twelve different directions to the gates of the city? There are so many questions that we probably will not find the answers to until we get there. One thing stands out clearly—the complexities of the New Jerusalem make it like no other dwelling place that has ever existed on this earth!

Eighteen

The Crowns

Throughout the Bible, God makes special promises to His children and to His chosen people. Clearly, God interacts with us as His family. More specifically, He views us as His children. From the moment we receive His Son as our Savior, we are identified as born again children. God presents Himself to us as our heavenly Father. *1 Peter, 1:23, "Being born again, not of corruptible seed, but of incorruptible, by the word of God, which liveth and abideth for ever."* Even Jesus, in teaching us how to pray, shows the family way to address God. *Matthew, 6:9, "After this manner therefore pray ye: Our Father which art in heaven, Hallowed be thy name."*

It is important to understand who we are in relationship to God. When we see God as our heavenly parent, it will clarify His expectations of us. His love for us demands obedience because He knows the eternal benefits of it. Sometimes, it seems like God's children have the idea that God will reward all of His children the same. Even though it is God's desire for all of His children to receive the best, the disobedience of some will not allow it. We understand the principle in our earthly families that when we are disobedient to our parents we are not rewarded in the same way as our siblings who have done what they were told.

> And ye have forgotten the exhortation which speaketh unto you as unto children, My son, despise not thou the chastening of the Lord, nor faint when thou art rebuked of him: For whom the Lord loveth he chasteneth, and scourgeth every son whom he receiveth. If ye endure chastening, God dealeth with you as with sons; for what son is he whom the father chasteneth not? But if ye be without chastisement, whereof all are partakers, then are ye bastards, and not sons. Furthermore we have had fathers of our flesh which corrected *us*, and we gave *them* reverence: shall we not much rather be in subjection unto the Father of spirits, and live? For they verily for a few days chastened *us* after their own pleasure; but he for *our* profit, that *we* might be partakers of his holiness. (Hebrews 12:5-10)

The desire of every child of God should be to actively live lives that bring honor and glory to our heavenly Father. Our aspiration in the Christian life should be to hear God say: "Well done good and faithful servant." Our motivation for living faithful lives should be love not merely to fulfill the commandments. Being obedient to God's commandments is important and a means of showing our love for the

One who gave His life for us! *John, 15:10-11, "If ye keep my commandments, ye shall abide in my love; even as I have kept my Father's commandments, and abide in his love. These things have I spoken unto you, that my joy might remain in you, and that your joy might be full."*

God has some amazing promises for His children. We receive some of them simply because we have been purchased by the blood of Jesus Christ. We became heirs of God because He birthed us into His family. A promise to live eternally in heavenly bodies also came by the birth. God has provided all of these things for us because we received the Lord Jesus Christ as our Savior.

Some of God's promises require more than the birth. The title of this book is *The High Calling of God* based on scriptures found in Philippians 3. Paul, by inspiration from God, talks about giving His life as a living sacrifice. He tells us of his desire to be more committed to a spiritual life. He admitted that there are things he hadn't attained unto even though he had been saved for a long time. *Philippians, 3:11-12, "If by any means I might attain unto the resurrection of the dead. Not as though I had already attained, either were already perfect: but I follow after, if that I may apprehend that for which also I am apprehended of Christ Jesus."* He wasn't talking about working for his salvation or indicating that he wouldn't be in the resurrection. He presents information about a *prize* God has for His children that will come only to those who persevere daily in sanctification of life.

Philippians, 3:13-14, "Brethren, I count not myself to have apprehended: but this one thing I do, forgetting those things which are behind, and reaching forth unto those things which are before, I press toward the mark for the prize of the high calling of God in Christ Jesus." There is a prize offered by God for His faithful children. Paul said it was the "High Calling!" *2 Timothy, 2:5, "And if a man also strive for masteries, yet is he not crowned, except he strive lawfully."*

Scripture reveals crowns that will be given to faithful children for different accomplishments. Not all the saved will have a crown. This may seem contrary to the teachings we have heard. We may have been encouraged that we will all cast our crowns at the feet of Jesus in heaven. There will be crowns in heaven that are cast at the feet of our Savior, but not by all of God's children. *Revelation, 4:10-11, "The four and twenty elders fall down before him that sat on the throne, and worship him that liveth for ever and ever, and cast their crowns before the throne, saying, Thou art worthy, O Lord, to receive glory and honour and power: for thou hast created all things, and for thy pleasure they are and were created."*

Let's look at the crowns and see what is required to get them. There are five different crowns mentioned, but I believe they all represent a position that will be given to the ones who qualify. In a kingdom, the king wears a crown and the wife of the king wears a crown. We have seen through our observations around the new heaven and new earth that not all of God's children live in the same place. There is a reason why some live in the New Jerusalem and some live on the outside. The promise of that special dwelling place was given to the church Jesus established during His personal ministry here on earth. In John 14, He told His espoused bride that He is going away to build a place for them to live in the eternal ages. He also promised that He would be coming back to receive them unto Himself that where He is, they would be also. As we consider the crowns, we will see that each one talks of some kind of commitment necessary to qualify for it. The Bible is clear that Jesus expects a high level of faithfulness from His espoused bride. Receiving a crown that will allow us to be the bride of the King ought to be a high motivator for dedicated Christian living.

The first crown we look at is one that is offered for enduring temptation. *James, 1:12, "Blessed is the man that endureth temptation: for when he is tried, he shall receive the crown of life, which the Lord hath promised to them that love him."* Because trials and temptations are such a huge part of living the Christian life, much is said about it. *James, 1:2-4, "My brethren, count it all joy when ye fall into divers temptations; Knowing this, that the trying of your faith worketh patience. But let patience have her perfect work, that ye may be perfect and entire, wanting nothing."* This crown comes to those who by faith walk in the Spirit, not fulfilling the lust of the flesh. Again, we see in this promise that it is not accomplished by following rules but is promised to those who love Jesus so much that they reject sin.

The next crown we consider is the one given to those who love the idea of Jesus returning. Every day is spent excitedly about His return. *2 Timothy, 4:7-8, "I have fought a good fight, I have finished my course, I have kept the faith: Henceforth there is laid up for me a crown of righteousness, which the Lord, the righteous judge, shall give me at that day: and not to me only, but unto all them also that love his appearing."* The qualification for this crown is simple. You don't have to be a pastor, evangelist, or a missionary—no not even a great theologian; you just have to be in love with Jesus. Remember, Jesus said, "If ye keep my commandments, ye shall abide in my love."

The martyr's crown will be given to those who died standing for the truths of the Lord Jesus Christ. *Revelation, 2:10, "Fear none of those things which thou shalt suffer: behold, the devil shall cast some of you into prison, that ye may be tried; and ye shall have tribulation ten days: be thou faithful unto death, and I will give thee a crown of life."* Most of us today do not have to worry about being arrested and thrown into prison for preaching the gospel. We are not in fear of our families or ourselves being killed for the truths that are preached in our churches each week. This has not always been the case. History tells us that the church suffered great persecution and millions died so we could have God's Word and the truths we have today!

The elder's crown is offered to faithful men who have been called by God to preach the word:

The elders which are among you I exhort, who am also an elder, and a witness of the sufferings of Christ, and also a partaker of the glory that shall be revealed: Feed the flock of God which is among you, taking the oversight thereof, not by constraint, but willingly; not for filthy lucre, but of a ready mind; Neither as being lords over God's heritage, but being ensamples to the flock. And when the chief Shepherd shall appear, ye shall receive a crown of glory that fadeth not away. (1 Peter 5:1-4)

God has requirements for receiving each of the crowns. This crown is only offered to men who have been faithful to their calling as a pastor, missionary, or any of the other duties that God has given to His chosen men.

Not everyone will be an *elder,* but God has a crown that everyone in the church can qualify for—loving the Lord God with all of our heart, and all of our soul; whether you are a man, a woman, or a child —God has a crown for His faithful, obedient children.

Finally, we look at the crown of the faithful. *Revelation, 3:11, "Behold, I come quickly: hold that fast which thou hast, that no man take thy crown."* Here Jesus encouraged the church of Philadelphia to take a stand for the doctrines that were once delivered to the saints. It's only by faith that we can be unwavering servants in His church. Sometimes, there will be pressure to compromise on the truth of God's Word, but we are told there is a crown for those who stand. *Hebrews, 10:23, "Let us hold fast the profession of our faith without wavering;*

(for he is faithful that promised." The other crowns have encouraged faithful Christian living. This crown speaks of standing for the doctrines God has left in His church as the guardians. *1 Timothy, 3:15, "But if I tarry long, that thou mayest know how thou oughtest to behave thyself in the house of God, which is the church of the living God, the pillar and ground of the truth."*

We have looked at five crowns. Devoted, sacrificial living attains the *Incorruptible Crown*, the *Crown of Rejoicing*, the *Martyr's Crown*, the *Crown of Righteousness,* and the *Elders Crown,* all of these are received by a walk of faith! Those who wear a crown will rule and reign with the bridegroom in the eternal ages!

Up to this section of the book, we have been trying to get a glimpse of what the new heaven and new earth will look like. Starting in the next section of the book, we are going to begin an examination of the bride and how she came about.

Nineteen
The Prize

Philippians, 3:14, "I press toward the mark for the prize of the high calling of God in Christ Jesus." If you haven't already figured it out, the "prize" is Jesus, the bridegroom. The day I was saved by the precious blood of my Savior Jesus Christ, I felt I had received the greatest gift that anyone could ever receive. I was on a spiritual high, the Holy Spirit of God had indwelt my human form, and I had become a new creation in Christ. *2 Corinthians, 5:17 "Therefore if any man be in Christ, he is a new creature: old things are passed away; behold, all things are become new."* At that time, I couldn't believe the gift God had given could get any better.

When I found out about the "High Calling of God in Christ Jesus," I was incredulous that God's grace could be even more amazing than I had ever believed possible. The opportunity to not only be born into the family of God but to win Christ in marriage would truly be the ultimate prize. In this chapter, we will look at the greatness of the *prize.*

Who is this Jesus who has been promised as the husband of the faithful espoused bride? *John, 1:1-3, "In the beginning was the Word, and the Word was with God, and the Word was God. The same was in the beginning with God. All things were made by him; and without him was not any thing made that was made."* We discover that He is God and that He was God in a human body while He was here on this earth. *John, 1:14, "And the Word was made flesh, and dwelt among us, (and we beheld his glory, the glory as of the only begotten of the Father,) full of grace and truth."* We also find that Jesus is the God of creation, everything made during the creation, including us, was made by Him.

When we are told that in the beginning, God created the heavens and the earth, He was there in Genesis doing the creating. On the sixth day when man was created, He was making that happen. When He saw that it was not good for Adam to be alone, He put him to sleep, took one of his ribs and made Eve. Sadly, He was there in the garden when Adam and Eve took the forbidden fruit disobeying God and bringing a sin curse upon all mankind.

After Adam and Eve had sinned, we began to see the depth of His love for them and for all mankind. *Ephesians, 1:4 "According as he hath chosen us in him before the foundation of the world, that we should be holy and without blame before him in love"* He already had a plan in place so no one would have to spend their eternity in hell. *2 Peter, 3:9: "The Lord is not slack concerning his promise, as some men count slackness; but is longsuffering to us-ward, not willing that any should perish, but that all should come to repentance."* When we see that He has a plan for all eternity to make a way of escape, we have a better understanding of the depth of His love as expressed in John 3:16.

Understanding Him in His work of creation gives us a greater appreciation for the church He established during His time on earth.

> *For by him were all things created, that are in heaven, and that are in earth, visible and invisible, whether they be thrones, or dominions, or principalities, or powers: all things were created by him, and for him: And he is before all things, and by him all things consist. And he is the head of the body, the church: who is the beginning, the firstborn from the dead; that in all things he might have the preeminence. For it pleased the Father that in him should all fulness dwell; (Colossians 1:16-19)*

Isaiah describes Him well:,

> For unto us a child is born, unto us a son is given: and the government shall be upon his shoulder: and his name shall be called Wonderful, Counseller, The mighty God, The everlasting Father, The Prince of Peace. Of the increase of *his* government and peace *there shall be* no end, upon the throne of David, and upon his kingdom, to order it, and to establish it with judgment and with justice from henceforth even for ever. The zeal of the LORD of hosts will perform this. **(Isaiah 9:6-7)**

We often hear these scriptures quoted at Christmas time as we are reminded that God came to this earth as a baby, humbling Himself that He might live in human form and make the ultimate human sacrifice.

These scriptures in Isaiah give us much more information about this bridegroom. He is the Prince of Peace. In this life, the characteristic of being a peacemaker is very desirable in a spouse. To be married to the one who has brought peace to mankind in every age is an exciting thought. We are also told that "the government shall be upon His shoulder." We look forward to the time when Christ will be the King of this present world during the thousand-year reign that is established after the seven-year tribulation. What makes this even more thrilling is that the faithful bride will reign with Him:

> *And I saw thrones, and they sat upon them, and judgment was given unto them: and I saw the souls of them that were beheaded for the witness of Jesus, and for the word of God, and which had not worshipped the beast, neither his image, neither had received his mark upon their foreheads, or in their hands; and they lived and reigned with Christ a thousand years. (Revelation 20:4)*

We further view the description of the bridegroom and find His name is Wonderful. Possibly, in this life, some women find a man who is portrayed as wonderful; no doubt, that has not always proven to be true. We know this report of Jesus is true because He is God and He is sinless and, perfect in every way. Just imagine the joy that shall fill the eternal ages as the bride lives in the wonderful mansion with her husband, whose name is Wonderful.

His name is also Counselor. Communication is often a big problem in earthly marriages. Wives get frustrated because their husbands do not talk with them or answer their questions. The love of Christ for His bride will make Him the perfect counselor because His abilities to know our every thought will administer the continual flow of information as we have questions. The very thought of living every day with Jesus who will answer every question we have ever had about anything we have wanted to know is so exhilarating!

The ability to protect and secure are also qualities that women seek in a husband. Never having to fear that our homes would be invaded or our possessions taken from us is a comforting thought.

Who will the bride be marrying? "**The Mighty God**" that's who! To understand that imperfect humans could ever have the opportunity to marry and live eternally with the mighty God is almost more than we can comprehend. If the scriptures did not reveal this great truth, we would never believe it.

The Bible, from Genesis to Revelation reveals the greatness of our God. He is the only way to salvation. He is the only means of being justified before our heavenly Father. He has shown His ability to protect His children from hungry lions, great armies, giants, and fiery furnaces. He created the universe and all that is in it in six days. He is the only God who would love even those who hated Him and tried to kill Him. Time and space would not allow us to describe all of His attributes and abilities.

The bridegroom is building a mansion, (New Jerusalem) for His wife—the church He started during His time here on Earth whom He promised to marry. That church has grown in every age and the size of His bride has increased. It started with twelve apostles but His promise of marriage has been given to every true church that has endured through time. The members of those churches who have loved Jesus with all their heart and have kept His commandments will live with Him in that special mansion He is now preparing.

He will be the bridegroom for those of His children who are willing to love Him with their lives and serve Him with everything they have:

> For this *man* was counted worthy of more glory than Moses, inasmuch as he who hath builded the house hath more honour than the house. For every house is builded by some *man*; but he that built all things *is* God. And Moses verily *was* faithful in all his house, as a servant, for a testimony of those things which were to be spoken after; But Christ as a son over his own house; whose house are we, if we hold fast the confidence and the rejoicing of the hope firm unto the end. (Hebrews 3:3-6)

Truthfully, the mark set before us is to gain the prize (the bridegroom). This is the ultimate opportunity for born again children of God. Will it take a full commitment to live or die for the cause of

Christ? Yes, it will take a full dedication every day of our lives, but it will be worth it! I want to live with the bridegroom in that beautiful mansion He has prepared for His bride. What about you, are you willing to pick up your cross and follow Him?

Twenty
The Bride's Journey

The first part of our book was spent trying to get some idea of how astonishing the eternal ages will be. We examined that unbelievable 1500-mile cubed city that the bridegroom is preparing for His bride. We examined the wonder of its construction and the marvelous colors that radiate from the walls and foundations. We saw gates made of single pearls that were so huge, the kings of the nations could walk through the openings without bending their heads. Then, we saw the angels that sat at each gate making sure that only those who had permission entered the city. Some questions were stirred in our minds about the angels being positioned at the gates throughout all eternity. Would they be the same angels or would it be different angels at different times? There are so many things to see and with our finite minds, we are only able to get a small taste of what it will be like.

My desire in this book was for us to get just a glimpse of the glory and magnitude of what God has in store for His faithful children. I wanted us to see how desirable it would be to live with Jesus as His bride in that great city. From this point on we will not have any imaginary *"angel guides"* to help us tour the future city. We are going to be examining the Scriptures to discover the origin of the bride, the purpose of the bride, and the qualifications to become a part of the greatest calling God ever made to His children. "The High Calling of God in Christ Jesus," is the subject of this book and the journey has just begun. My hope is, that you continue with me, as we see what God has to say about this *"High Calling."*

The First Introduction

Then there arose a question between some of John's disciples and the Jews about purifying. And they came unto John, and said unto him, Rabbi, he that was with thee beyond Jordan, to whom thou barest witness, behold, the same baptizeth, and all men come to him. John answered and said, A man can receive nothing, except it be given him from heaven. Ye yourselves bear me witness, that I said, I am not the Christ, but that I am sent before him. He that hath the bride is the bridegroom: but the friend of the bridegroom, which standeth and heareth him, rejoiceth greatly because of the bridegroom's voice: this my joy therefore is fulfilled. He must increase, but I must decrease. He that cometh from above is above all: he that is of the earth is earthly, and speaketh of the earth: he that cometh from heaven is above all. And what he hath seen and

heard, that he testifieth; and no man receiveth his
testimony. He that hath received his testimony hath set
to his seal that God is true. For he whom God hath sent
speaketh the words of God: for God giveth not the
Spirit by measure unto him. The Father loveth the Son,
and hath given all things into his hand. He that
believeth on the Son hath everlasting life: and he that
believeth not the Son shall not see life; but the wrath of
God abideth on him. (John 3:25-36)

John's disciples came to him with a question about Jesus' authority to baptize converts. John tells these men, "The authority of Jesus comes from God!" The next piece of information he disclosed was totally new to this Jewish congregation! Jesus is a "bridegroom" and He has a "bride" with Him. He further uncovered new information; John revealed that he is the "friend of the bridegroom!" This is not just shocking information for John's disciples but for all of us who study the Bible.

The Old Testament talks about God's relationship with Israel as a wife. Israel's unfaithfulness to God caused Him to declare a divorce. The only place in the Old Testament that a reference to Christ and a bride is implied is in Song of Solomon. Some present the tabernacle as a type of the church as the bride of Christ. These examples very well may teach about Christ and His bride but there did not seem to be any clear teaching concerning an engagement of Messiah to a people at His coming. John's disciples got the first clear statements about Messiah being a bridegroom and the bride already being with Him.

The Friend of the Bridegroom

Who is the "friend"? The simple answer seems to be John the Baptist! What does he mean by this statement? The idea of John being the friend is revealed as an Old Testament concept or practice involving the choosing of a bride for a Hebrew son. Genesis chapter 24, gives the case of Abraham who sent his head servant to find a wife for his son, Isaac and how he found Rachel and brought her back to marry him. This was the custom of those times where the friend of the bridegroom went before to find and prepare a bride for a son. Viewing this custom being carried out by John the Baptist for Jesus is very beautiful spiritually when it is presented in New Testament scripture.

First, we see that the Father chose the friend to go before His son to prepare a wife. *John 1:6-8, "There was a man sent from God, whose name was John. The same came for a witness, to bear witness of the Light, that all men through him might believe. He was not that Light, but was sent to bear witness of that Light."* The whole life of John reveals him to be special above all others. He was God's chosen one. First, we see his birth to parents who were past the age for bearing children—like Abraham and Sarah. Then we see his father Zacharias who was made unable to speak until John was born. After regaining his speech he confirmed that his child would be called Joh, contrary to the usual custom of naming a Hebrew son. Jesus said there were no others born who were greater than John. *Luke 7:28, "For I say unto you, Among those that are born of women there is not a greater prophet than John the Baptist: but he that is least in the kingdom of God is greater than he."* John, like Jesus, did not begin his ministry until he was 30 years old. Under Hebrew law, one cannot assume the position of priest or prophet until this age. This is required as Jesus is to become the High Priest; John is the last of the Old Testament prophets and ends the age of the law covenant. *Luke 16:16, "The law and the prophets were until John: since that time the kingdom of God is preached, and every man presseth into it."*

John's purpose for being the precursor to Jesus is to prepare the people who would become Jesus' church and ultimately His bride. *Luke 1:17, "And he shall go before him in the spirit and power of Elias, to turn the hearts of the fathers to the children, and the disobedient to the wisdom of the just; to make ready a people prepared for the Lord."* John was six months older than Jesus and both of them began their ministries at the age of 30. John had been preaching repentance and the exciting news that the kingdom of heaven was about to begin. Souls were saved and received this new rite of baptism. Some, who began to follow, were already saved, but they were baptized as well because they wanted to be part of these new people who would represent their God.

John only went to the Jewish people and had no ministry with the Gentiles. John, like Jesus, was still under the law that was only given to Israel. The door, opening the right of entrance to the Gentiles, did not happen until after Christ's death on the cross. John's whole purpose, as he stated in John 3, was to bear witness of the light who was about to establish His kingdom people. John was a saved man, who had been called by God to prepare the bride for Jesus. John himself was not baptized and didn't become a part of the church Jesus was about to bring into existence. He would not be a part of the bride of Christ. He will be the friend of the bridegroom and no doubt, God has some great rewards for him in the eternal ages. *Luke 7:28, "For I say unto you, Among those that are born of women there is not a greater prophet than John the Baptist: but he that is least in the kingdom of God is greater than he."*

John began something unheard of by the Jews, the act of baptism. God made sure that Israel knew he was special by the events that surrounded his birth, his life, and his ministry. God wanted the Jews, of the old covenant, to receive His heaven-sent baptism. That baptism revealed John's authority from God to administer it. Baptism prepared those who received it to be a part of Christ's church and for those who followed Jesus to be a part of His bride. When Jesus was questioned about His authority, He referred those doubters to the authority of John:

> *The baptism of John, whence was it? from heaven, or of men?*
> *And they reasoned with themselves, saying, If we shall*
> *say, From heaven; he will say unto us, Why did ye not*

then believe him? But if we shall say, Of men; we fear

the people; for all hold John as a prophet. And they

answered Jesus, and said, We cannot tell. And he said

unto them, Neither tell I you by what authority I do

these things. (Matthew 21:25-27)

When examining John's life and ministry, we could say that his greatest call from God was to "make ready" a people prepared for the Lord. When those men and women who followed John saw Jesus come on the scene, they were confused. They saw the disciples of Jesus baptizing more than John, and they were not sure if this was right. When they came to John, he assured them that Jesus was the Lamb of God who takes away the sin of the world. He encouraged them that they needed to follow Jesus. He made it clear that his joy was full, and that being the friend of the bridegroom was his great privilege from God. He made it clear that Jesus was the bridegroom, and the church who was following Him was the bride:

Then came to him the disciples of John, saying, Why do we and

the Pharisees fast oft, but thy disciples fast not? And

Jesus said unto them, Can the children of the

bridechamber mourn, as long as the bridegroom is with

them? but the days will come, when the bridegroom

shall be taken from them, and then shall they fast.

(Matthew 9:14-15)

John, like the head servant of Abraham, was sent to make ready a bride for God's Son. Isaac was excited when he saw Rachel, the woman chosen to be His bride. Jesus was excited when He found the people that the "man sent from God," had made ready for Him. Immediately after His temptation in the wilderness, Jesus began calling out the men who would form the "first church":

From that time Jesus began to preach, and to say, Repent: for the kingdom of heaven is at hand. And Jesus, walking by the sea of Galilee, saw two brethren, Simon called Peter, and Andrew his brother, casting a net into the sea: for they were fishers. And he saith unto them, Follow me, and I will make you fishers of men. And they straightway left their nets, and followed him. And going on from thence, he saw other two brethren, James the son of Zebedee, and John his brother, in a ship with Zebedee their father, mending their nets; and he called them. And they immediately left the ship and their father, and followed him. (Matthew 4:17-22)

This church was formed and working when John's disciples asked him, by what authority was Jesus baptizing? At this time, John referred to Jesus' church as the bride. We will look closer at this church as we continue in the coming chapters.

Twenty-One
Who Approved It?

Throughout the ministry of Jesus, the Jewish religious leaders questioned Him about who was authorizing Him to do the miracles He did and to teach the things He taught! *Matthew 21:23, "And when he was come into the temple, the chief priests and the elders of the people came unto him as he was teaching, and said, By what authority doest thou these things? and who gave thee this authority?"* Our study of the bride of Christ deserves a look at, "Who approved it?" When a man announces he is going to marry a woman, often, the question is; "Did you get her parent's permission or approval?"

From the beginning of man's existence, God has always been the authority. God is sovereign, no one tells God what to do. God the Father, Son, and the Holy Spirit have not changed. He still reigns over all and is the power that operates all things. From Genesis to Revelation, God is the authority delegating His power and authority to the people who would represent His name.

Understanding that God is the sovereign authority for every doctrine and teaching in the Bible helps us see why this bride needs approval. The subject of the bride of Christ is about God giving approval for a people of His creation to marry His Son and live in eternity with Him. We have concerns for our earthly children about their choice of life partners. Likewise, God will accept only the best for His Son. Sometimes, we are disappointed with the decisions our children make in choosing a mate. There will be no mistakes about who will be the wife of Jesus Christ. God is sovereign; He sets the rules for entrance into the marriage of His Son. Only those who submit to God's plan will be a part of the bride of Christ. Just as God's plan for being born again only happens when meeting God's requirements, the same is true for being a part of the bride.

A Chain of Authority

In the last chapter, we saw that John the Baptist was God's chosen man to prepare the material for the church Jesus would establish. This church was going to be the espoused bride of Jesus. That is why it is so important to examine the lineage of God's authority on her.

What we are going to see in this chapter is the birth of a church. The establishment of this body is by the authority of God and according to His eternal purposes. We must understand that this church is not mystical or invisible. It is a living visible body that was formed from the saved, baptized people that John the Baptist prepared for Jesus! Those who became a part of this church had to meet God's requirements. They had to be born again. John made it clear to the

Pharisees that they had to show the fruits of repentance before he would baptize them. The only baptism that was acceptable to bring them into this new church, was the baptism administered by John. He was the only one "sent from God," which reveals proper authority in baptism.

We understand that even Jesus had to go to John to receive the *heaven-approved* act. Before Jesus began His earthly ministry, John baptized Him. John didn't want to baptize Jesus because he knew He was God. He didn't believe he was even worthy to tie His shoes. Jesus explains to John that an example is being set. When we look back today, we see Jesus going to the man who had the authority from God to baptize. Jesus was baptized by immersion with God's authority behind it. The men Jesus began calling out to be part of His church had to have John's baptism. Without this baptism, they couldn't qualify to be a part of the body of Christ—, His church.

When Jesus began to call out the men who would comprise His first church, He emphasized that a full commitment of their lives was necessary to become His church. He told them He was going to make them "fishers of men" and shortly thereafter, He empowered them with authority from heaven to baptize the new converts. It needs to be understood that the church the Bible speaks of is not an invisible body of all the saved of all ages.

It is easy to see the succession of authority in the chosen people of God in the Old Testament because it literally happened by the birthing process. Through Adam and the faithful patriarchs, we see the passing of authority going through the genealogies of the chosen people. As we look at Israel, we have no problem understanding her authority. The passing of authority was by the people of God dying and being replaced by new bodies. Following the genealogies, we see God delivering His Son at the right time and place to fulfill His promise of a Messiah, a Redeemer! As messed up as Israel was when Jesus began His ministry, He did not sidestep the issue of who had the authority. For three and one-half years the church Jesus established labored under the authority of the Word that was given to the chosen people Israel. They kept the Sabbath, and they were subject to the law in every way. *Matthew 10:5-7, "These twelve Jesus sent forth, and commanded them, saying, Go not into the way of the Gentiles, and into any city of the Samaritans enter ye not: But go rather to the lost sheep of the house of Israel. And as ye go, preach, saying, The kingdom of heaven is at hand.".* Jesus was and is God, but He knew that until the law was fulfilled, you couldn't step outside the authority of God. Even John the Baptist would not have been there to baptize Jesus if the succession of authority through the birthing process had not been established there.

The beginning of the succession of New Testament authority is seen as we first look at John the Baptist. *John 1:6 "There was a man sent from God, whose name was John."* Everything about John is special. He was the forerunner to Christ and the new covenant that was about to do away with the old one. Israel was not easily going to accept these new changes. God confirmed the authority He had given to John by his birth, his special abilities, etc. He does all of these amazing things to John so Israel would accept his authority. Jesus recognized the authority of John when He walked over sixty-five miles through the Judean desert to receive John's baptism:

> *Then cometh Jesus from Galilee to Jordan unto John, to be baptized of him. But John forbad him, saying, I have need to be baptized of thee, and comest thou to me? And Jesus answering said unto him, Suffer it to be so now: for thus it becometh us to fulfil all righteousness. Then he suffered him. (Matthew 3:13-15)*

John thought that the authority of Christ ought to supersede his. John did not want to baptize Jesus because he knew Jesus was God. Jesus told John that he must do this so people would understand what "scriptural" baptism involves. Jesus taught John about "authority." God the Father, and God the Holy Spirit revealed their pleasure in Jesus' recognition of John's authority as Jesus came up out of the water. *Matthew 3:16-17, "And Jesus, when he was baptized, went up straightway out of the water: and, lo, the heavens were opened unto him, and he saw the Spirit of God descending like a dove, and lighting upon him: And lo a voice from heaven, saying, This is my beloved Son, in whom I am well pleased."* Today, we have the scripture, which says, *"There was a man sent from God, whose name was John" (John*

1:6). From this, we can see the authority behind John's baptism. No doubt, John knew that God had called him and had given him this new ordinance. He was a priest under the law covenant and God instructed him to do something that had never been done before. Baptism was a new commandment. He struggled with baptizing Jesus because he probably didn't understand his calling was from the Godhead. Jesus was part of the issuing authority, thus, Jesus was not going to usurp authority over Himself. After receiving baptism from the man with authority, Jesus began His ministry.

In the fourth chapter of Matthew, we see Jesus call out those who would be His body, His church. Jesus exercised His authority as He gives it to the church. John was still living at this point, but there is no question in his mind the authority had passed to Christ, as he is soon to die:

> *After these things came Jesus and his disciples into the land of Judaea; and there he tarried with them, and baptized. And John also was baptizing in AEnon near to Salim, because there was much water there: and they came, and were baptized. For John was not yet cast into prison. Then there arose a question between some of John's disciples and the Jews about purifying. And they came unto John, and said unto him, Rabbi, he that was with thee beyond Jordan, to whom thou barest witness, behold, the same baptizeth, and all men come to him. John answered and said, A man can receive nothing,*

except it be given him from heaven. (John 3:22-27)

The Greek word that means to send with authority is not used here but context certainly reveals that John was talking about the authority of Jesus to baptize. Original languages enhance our studying, but if we try to produce doctrine based primarily on word studies, we will fail ourselves. We should study the Word letting context teach us. I might inject at this point that any study without prayer and leadership of the Holy Spirit will take us in the wrong directions.

We continue our Bible examination of the doctrine of authority by going to *John 4:1-2, "When therefore the Lord knew how the Pharisees had heard that Jesus made and baptized more disciples than John, (Though Jesus himself baptized not, but his disciples),"* These verses show that the authority for baptism had been moved to the church. Jesus is given credit for these baptisms, but He did not administer them, He gave the authority to perform them to the church. It is clear, the Pharisees understood who had given the church their authority. In Matthew 10:5-6, Jesus sent the church with His authority to preach. The authority is limited to go only to Israel. The reason, of course, as we previously stated is that the church was still under the law covenant given to Israel.

The issue of authority is nothing new, Jesus was questioned about authority in *Matthew 21:23-27:*

And when he was come into the temple, the chief priests and the elders of the people came unto him as he was teaching,

and said, By what authority doest thou these things?
and who gave thee this authority? And Jesus answered
and said unto them, I also will ask you one thing, which
if ye tell me, I in like wise will tell you by what authority
I do these things. The baptism of John, whence was it?
from heaven, or of men? And they reasoned with
themselves, saying, If we shall say, From heaven; he
will say unto us, Why did ye not then believe him? But if
we shall say, Of men; we fear the people; for all hold
John as a prophet. And they answered Jesus, and said,
We cannot tell. And he said unto them, Neither tell I
you by what authority I do these things. (Matthew
21:23-27)

What's going on here? Why doesn't Jesus tell these Pharisee's about authority?

God intended for us to study to learn the deep things about His ways. Notice the conversation between Jesus and His disciples:

And the disciples came, and said unto him, Why speakest thou
unto them in parables? He answered and said unto
them, Because it is given unto you to know the
mysteries of the kingdom of heaven, but to them it is
not given. For whosoever hath, to him shall be given,
and he shall have more abundance: but whosoever
hath not, from him shall be taken away even that he
hath. Therefore speak I to them in parables: because
they seeing see not; and hearing they hear not, neither

do they understand. And in them is fulfilled the prophecy of Esaias, which saith, By hearing ye shall hear, and shall not understand; and seeing ye shall see, and shall not perceive: For this people's heart is waxed gross, and their ears are dull of hearing, and their eyes they have closed; lest at any time they should see with their eyes, and hear with their ears, and should understand with their heart, and should be converted, and I should heal them. But blessed are your eyes, for they see: and your ears, for they hear. For verily I say unto you, That many prophets and righteous men have desired to see those things which ye see, and have not seen them; and to hear those things which ye hear, and have not heard them. (Matthew 13:10-17)

Jesus told His church that He would send the Holy Spirit to her to teach them things that those outside the church could not see or understand:

Howbeit when he, the Spirit of truth, is come, he will guide you into all truth: for he shall not speak of himself; but whatsoever he shall hear, that shall he speak: and he will shew you things to come. He shall glorify me: for he shall receive of mine, and shall shew it unto you. All things that the Father hath are mine: therefore said I, that he shall take of mine, and shall shew it unto you. (John 16:13-15)

Only those who are willing to allow the Holy Spirit to teach them will have the eyes to see. These Pharisees did not want to admit that John's baptism had authority behind it. They did not want to admit that the church Jesus had established had its authority from God. If they would have admitted that His ministry (the building of His church) was from God, they would have had to admit their guilt in not being a part of it.

Once we understand that Jesus built His visible church while He was here on the earth, many other scriptures open our eyes to see God's authority in everything.

Twenty-Two
The New Covenant

God has made a new covenant with His church and according to *Hebrews 8:6-7,* it's a better covenant, *"But now hath he obtained a more excellent ministry, by how much also he is the mediator of a better covenant, which was established upon better promises. For if that first covenant had been faultless, then should no place have been sought for the second."* The first covenant was given to a particular people (Israel), it was necessary for them to perpetuate through the birthing process for that covenant to remain in effect. The same thing is true with the new covenant; it was given to chosen people (not to individuals, but to the body that Jesus established, His church). For the covenant to still be in effect today, the birthing process has been going on in every age. Jesus promised in Matt 16:18, that the gates of hell would not prevail against that body He has established. In Matt. 28:18-20, He gave that body the authority to make disciples, baptize, and teach His people to observe His commandments. He also promised the church He would be with her in every age. He revealed that the birthing process would continue until He comes again. In Ephesians

3:21, God says He gets glory through the church and would do so in every age. This shows that the promises made to that original body would extend to every age. This could not happen if the succession of churches were not a reality.

We continue to see the authority and perpetuity of the church as we view its establishment. It started when Jesus began calling out the material that John had prepared. *Luke 1:17, "And he shall go before him in the spirit and power of Elias, to turn the hearts of the fathers to the children, and the disobedient to the wisdom of the just; to make ready a people prepared for the Lord."* The issue is not the exact point of origin (seashore, mountain top, Jordan River, etc.) but to see that it began during Jesus' ministry, by His authority. We also see that this authority was passed to His church. By the time we get to Matt 16:18-20, the church is in existence:

> *And I say also unto thee, That thou art Peter, and upon this rock I will build my church; and the gates of hell shall not prevail against it. And I will give unto thee the keys of the kingdom of heaven: and whatsoever thou shalt bind on earth shall be bound in heaven: and whatsoever thou shalt loose on earth shall be loosed in heaven. Then charged he his disciples that they should tell no man that he was Jesus the Christ. (Matthew 16:18-20)*

Notice context, He is talking to His church telling them that she is built on Him. Giving assurance that this earthly spiritual body that He has established will not go out of existence. She will perpetuate in every age.

In these verses, He gives the church authority to loose and bind. The church has no authority to bind people in salvation. Salvation is from God and has nothing to do with the church, (though we must preach it, and a person must be saved to be part of it). The church also has no authority to loose anyone from salvation. These verses are revealing the authority from God to bind people into the church or make them members by the authority given us by Christ. It also gives us the authority to loose those who have been bound or exclude them from the church by the authority of Christ.

It is evident, that this is the subject as we further see Jesus instructing the church on how to handle disorderly members:

> *Moreover if thy brother shall trespass against thee, go and tell him his fault between thee and him alone: if he shall hear thee, thou hast gained thy brother. But if he will not hear thee, then take with thee one or two more, that in the mouth of two or three witnesses every word may be established. And if he shall neglect to hear them, tell it unto the church: but if he neglect to hear the church, let him be unto thee as an heathen man and a publican. Verily I say unto you,* **Whatsoever ye shall bind on earth shall be bound in heaven: and whatsoever ye shall loose on earth shall be loosed in**

> **heaven**. *Again I say unto you, That if two of you shall agree on earth as touching any thing that they shall ask, it shall be done for them of my Father which is in heaven. <u>For where two or three are gathered together in my name, there am I in the midst of them.</u> (Matthew 18:15-20)*

(Notice this underlined portion of scripture is not talking about how to start a church but about the authority of the church when involved in discipline.)

We also see the extension of this authority revealed in the Corinthian Church:

> *1 Corinthians 5:11-13 But now I have written unto you not to keep company, if any man that is called a brother be a fornicator, or covetous, or an idolater, or a railer, or a drunkard, or an extortioner; with such an one no not to eat. For what have I to do to judge them also that are without? do not ye judge them that are within? But them that are without God judgeth. Therefore put away from among yourselves that wicked person.*

> *1 Corinthians 6:1-3 Dare any of you, having a matter against another, go to law before the unjust, and not before the saints? Do ye not know that the saints shall judge the world? and if the world shall be judged by you, are ye unworthy to judge the smallest matters? Know ye not that we shall judge angels? how much more things*

that pertain to this life?

The reason true New Testament churches vote on someone becoming a member of the church is because Christ gave the authority to the church to bind. He didn't give that authority to a preacher, committee, deacons, or anyone else, except the church. Scriptures like this give instructions on how to operate in the Lord's church. It throws out the idea that the church can be a universal body made up of all the saved. How could such a body ever operate, how could they "loose" or "bind" members?

The church decides who is a qualified candidate for membership, no one else. The church looks at the scriptural qualifications (Are you saved? Do you want to make a full commitment to Christ? Are you willing to abide by all of the teachings in the Bible?) It is just as foolish to say the church has no right to vote on excluding a member, as it is to say the church has no right to vote on receiving one. Anyone who would get offended by having a church vote to receive him or her is showing right up front that they have a problem with the church having authority over their lives. They would have trouble with the church telling them that they can't drink socially , cuss, tell dirty stories, gamble, use drugs, and the list goes on. God's covenant with the church requires the full commitment of those who enter into it. *Ephesians 5:25-27, "Husbands, love your wives, even as Christ also loved the church, and gave himself for it; That he might sanctify and cleanse it with the washing of water by the word, That he might present it to himself a glorious church, not having spot, or wrinkle, or any such thing; but that it should be holy and without blemish."* We further view the passing of authority as we see Jesus giving it to the church in *Matthew 28:18-20, "And Jesus came and spake unto them, saying, All power is given unto me in heaven and in earth. Go ye therefore, and teach all nations, baptizing them in the name of the Father, and of the Son, and of the Holy Ghost: Teaching them to observe all things whatsoever I have commanded you: and, lo, I am with you alway, even unto the end of the world. Amen."* In the eighteenth verse, Jesus sets the stage revealing by what authority He gave the commission to His church. When He says, "Go ye," we see the authority given to the church. The church has the authority to evangelize the whole world. She has the authority to baptize and the authority to teach her members to practice all of the things Jesus taught while He was with them.

It was to the visible church of Jesus Christ that the commission was given. That to which the commission was given and the church has the promise of continued existence to the end of the world, for after giving the command, the Lord said, "Lo, I am with you alway, even to the end of the world." Those to whom He spoke lived only a few years after this commission was given, hence, the Master could not have made such a promise to them as individuals. It was to them collectively as the body of Christ, His visible church. The church was the only one having authority to baptize, it follows that all baptisms administered without church authority are not accepted by God as legitimate. For this reason, true churches have, in all ages, refused to recognize the baptisms of those who were not baptized by the authority of a scriptural church. Scriptural baptism is the immersion of a saved person by the authority of a scriptural church.

Some would say the church was not started until the Day of Pentecost when the Holy Spirit baptized and empowered them. The scriptures we have examined thus far would show this teaching to be false. In Matthew18, where Jesus told His church how to handle conflicts among Christian brothers and sisters, He instructed them that when they couldn't resolve a problem to tell it to the church. If the church was not started until Pentecost, how is this possible? *1 Corinthians 12:28, "And God hath set some in the church, first apostles, secondarily prophets, thirdly teachers, after that miracles, then gifts of healings, helps, governments, diversities of tongues."* This verse says that God set apostles in the church—this was one of the first things Jesus did when He began His ministry. The reason some struggle to admit that Jesus started the church during His pre-crucifixion ministry is because it limits who has authority to baptize and who is qualified to be a part of the bride of Christ. We will continue to examine how a clear lineage of perpetuity and authority are seen in the Bible in our next chapter.

Twenty-Three
Loving Jesus

How important is faithful living? Often, when churches emphasize the need for full commitment, they get labeled a "legalistic church." Could it be that the objectors are people who don't want anyone controlling their lives? The truth is, when we make a full commitment to Jesus by being obedient to His command for baptism and entering into His church, He wants full control. An interesting discourse was held with Jesus and His disciples:

> *Then Jesus said unto them, Verily, verily, I say unto you, Except ye eat the flesh of the Son of man, and drink his blood, ye have no life in you. Whoso eateth my flesh, and drinketh my blood, hath eternal life; and I will raise him up at the last day. For my flesh is meat indeed, and my blood is drink indeed. He that eateth my flesh, and drinketh my blood, dwelleth in me, and I in him. (John 6:53-56)*

Wow! I think many of us would be shocked by a message like this. Can you imagine your pastor getting up next Sunday and presenting such a message?

Jesus was unwavering on the challenge He had put to His disciples. *John 6:57, "As the living Father hath sent me, and I live by the Father: so he that eateth me, even he shall live by me."* He was not talking to these disciples about being born again; He was talking about the sanctification of life, (separating ourselves from the world.) Jesus wanted His church to make Him the center of their lives and of their decisions. Being born again does not take any commitment. We repent and believe in Jesus' death for us, and God, the Holy Spirit, births us into His family. These disciples knew He was asking them to give up some things and take on some new commitments. *John 6:60, "Many therefore of his disciples, when they had heard this, said, This is an hard saying; who can hear it?"*

Jesus knew the Christian life would not be easy, but He also knew the eternal benefits would be worth the dedication. *John 6:61, "When Jesus knew in himself that his disciples murmured at it, he said unto them, Doth this offend you?"* He wanted them to know that the fleshly side of life was not going to profit them. *John 6:63, "It is the spirit that quickeneth; the flesh profiteth nothing: the words that I speak unto you, they are spirit, and they are life."* Jesus presented the qualifications for service to these disciples because He loved them.

As a pastor, I know how discouraging it is when someone gets up and leaves a service while I am preaching. Jesus taught us to preach the truth whether we are received well or not. He knew what it was like to be rejected. *John 6:66, "From that time many of his disciples went back, and walked no more with him."* After these people left, He asked His church if these words were going to cause them to leave as well? *John 6:67-68, "Then said Jesus unto the twelve, Will ye also go away? Then Simon Peter answered him, Lord, to whom shall we go? thou hast the words of eternal life. "* Peter had the right answer, "to whom shall we go?" When we love Jesus like He loves us we will not go anywhere else, and we won't balk at things He sets before us to do!

In another discourse with His called out assembly, He assured them that they were "**His Church**" !

> *And Jesus answered and said unto him, Blessed art thou, Simon Barjona: for flesh and blood hath not revealed it unto thee, but my Father which is in heaven. And I say also unto thee, That thou art Peter, and upon this rock I will build my church; and the gates of hell shall not prevail against it. And I will give unto thee the keys of the kingdom of heaven: and whatsoever thou shalt bind on earth shall be bound in heaven: and whatsoever thou shalt loose on earth shall be loosed in heaven.*
> *(Matthew 16:17-19)*

As Jesus gave His church the information that He is the "Rock" and the church is built on Him, He informed them of the hard job they would have governing His church. He further let them know of His pending death in Jerusalem. Peter didn't want to hear this information about Jesus leaving them. Jesus informed all of them that great things would be expected from them:

> Then said Jesus unto his disciples, If any man will come after me,
> let him deny himself, and take up his cross, and follow
> me. For whosoever will save his life shall lose it: and
> whosoever will lose his life for my sake shall find it. For
> what is a man profited, if he shall gain the whole world,
> and lose his own soul? or what shall a man give in
> exchange for his soul? For the Son of man shall come in
> the glory of his Father with his angels; and then he
> shall reward every man according to his works.
> (Matthew 16:24-27)

Jesus is not talking to lost people about what they will lose if they are not saved before they die. He is talking to His saved, baptized, church.

He revealed His expectations for the body that would represent Him in every age. "If you are going to follow me, you will have to deny yourself." Denying our flesh is the struggle of Christianity. We wake each day knowing our fleshly nature is going to want things that are ungodly. *1 John 2:16, "For all that is in the world, the lust of the flesh, and the lust of the eyes, and the pride of life, is not of the Father, but is of the world."* He said we would have to "take up our cross and follow Him." He was letting us know that being a Christian meant we would have to be Christlike. He informs us that if we decide to save our lives, we will lose them. Again, He is not talking about us keeping our salvation, only God can do that! The word "soul" means life; He is talking about us living dedicated, consecrated lives for Him after we are saved. The question in Matthew 16, "What shall a man give in exchange for his soul?" is asking us if there is anything in this world worth giving up our Christian walk for. Jesus encourages His church by saying that He is coming again and when He comes, He will reward every man, woman, boy, and girl according to their works.

As we viewed the *great* city Jesus prepared for His bride in the first part of this book, it was amazing beyond words. Now, we realize it is the righteousness of the saints that will give the bride her garments and entrance to that city. This makes these verses seem much more real. *Matthew 16:26-27, "For what is a man profited, if he shall gain the whole world, and lose his own soul? or what shall a man give in exchange for his soul? For the Son of man shall come in the glory of his Father with his angels; and then he shall reward every man according to his works."*

Yes, our works matter. *James 2:17-18, "Even so faith, if it hath not works, is dead, being alone. Yea, a man may say, Thou hast faith, and I have works: shew me thy faith without thy works, and I will shew thee my faith by my works."* We know that salvation is not by works of righteousness which we have done. Jesus said each of us would be rewarded according to our works. James explains that without works, there is no evidence of our faith. The idea that one can be saved by the grace and love of God and then live a disobedient life without consequences is unbiblical. Often, our human reasoning will tell us the disobedient, saved person will lose their salvation this too is unbiblical.

Jesus gave a kingdom parable in *Matthew 25:14-15, "For the kingdom of heaven is as a man travelling into a far country, who called his own servants, and delivered unto them his goods. And unto one he gave five talents, to another two, and to another one; to every man according to his several ability; and straightway took his journey."* This parable is not about three men who were working to get to heaven. The idea, taught by some in the religious world, that our works, good and bad, would be weighed on a scale at death to see if we make it to heaven is false. Saint Peter is not waiting at heaven's gate to determine who has done enough to get in. Jesus settled our destiny to heaven when He paid for the sins of all mankind by the shedding of His blood. Everyone who accepts His free gift of eternal life is guaranteed to live throughout eternity in heaven. That is settled here on earth before we die.

These three men represent three saved men who were in the Lord's church. They were part of His kingdom people. They represent God giving to each of His children certain abilities. Clearly, not everyone has the same capabilities, but God expects each of us to use what we have to glorify Him. Some people have musical talents; some have higher levels of intelligence, and some have skills that are peculiar to them. God is an equal opportunity employer. This parable reveals God's pleasure in those who were obedient with what He had given them. It also discloses His displeasure with the children of disobedience.

Matthew 7:13-14, "Enter ye in at the strait gate: for wide is the gate, and broad is the way, that leadeth to destruction, and many there be which go in thereat: Because strait is the gate, and narrow is the way, which leadeth unto life, and few there be that find it." Jesus is teaching His church in this seventh chapter about Christian living. The idea of putting others first is the theme. These scriptures are not about being born again but about the sanctification of life. The encouragement to the church is to walk a narrow path. Often, when churches take a narrow stand on the doctrines of the Bible, they are labeled as narrow or inflexible. Sadly, verse 14 describes the pattern that is often taken by God's children. All have not obeyed the way of righteousness. Part of "picking up our cross" and following Jesus is about entering into the straight gate.

Revelation 19:7, "Let us be glad and rejoice, and give honour to him: for the marriage of the Lamb is come, and his wife hath made herself ready." To be a part of the bride of Christ, we have to be working to make ourselves ready for our coming Savior. The idea of meeting the bridegroom in the air as the bride is such an exciting visualization of our futures. To believe that God would be willing to allow you or me into the bride of His Son is humbling. He makes it obvious that we will be part of that chosen group not because we are great, but because we humbled ourselves and followed His will.

Because the foolishness of God is wiser than men; and the weakness of God is stronger than men. For ye see your calling, brethren, how that not many wise men after the flesh, not many mighty, not many noble, are called: But God hath chosen the foolish things of the world to confound the wise; and God hath chosen the weak things of the world to confound the things which are mighty; And base things of the world, and things which are despised, hath God chosen, yea, and things which are not, to bring to nought things that are: That no flesh should glory in his presence. (1 Corinthians 1:25-29)

We, like Paul, must put our eyes on the prize before us, not counting the things of this world with any esteem. We need to be so in love with Jesus and live every day as a new opportunity to advance His cause: *"And be found in him, not having mine own righteousness, which is of the law, but that which is through the faith of Christ, the righteousness which is of God by faith: That I may know him, and the power of his resurrection, and the fellowship of his sufferings, being made conformable unto his death"* (Philippians 3:9-10).

Twenty-Four
The Mission Way

We have been looking at the church Jesus built during His personal ministry and seeing the importance of God's authority in every phase of it. This book is about the "High Calling of God,' a look at the bride of Christ. Understanding how the bride came into existence, and God's requirements to be a part of her is founded in the doctrine of authority. Jesus established the first church and then made some promises to her about her perpetuating throughout all ages. This meant the Jerusalem church was not going to be the only church like her. A continuing connection from all true churches would historically connect them to the church in Jerusalem that Jesus founded. When we talk about "authority" in essence, we talk about the sovereignty of God. We do not decide what a church is, God tells us how to identify His church.

In the last chapter, we traced the beginning of the new covenant to John the Baptist, the man "sent" from God. John did not start the new church; he was just the authority from God to prepare the material. We then saw Jesus come to the only one with authority from

God and received His baptism from John. After Jesus was baptized, God put His stamp of approval on it. *Matthew 3:16-17 "And Jesus, when he was baptized, went up straightway out of the water: and, lo, the heavens were opened unto him, and he saw the Spirit of God descending like a dove, and lighting upon him: And lo a voice from heaven, saying, This is my beloved Son, in whom I am well pleased."* Jesus was now ready to form His church. He called out the twelve apostles who had John's baptism and gave them the authority to start baptizing the new converts. The twelve apostles were not the only ones who became part of this first church. On the day of Pentecost, we saw 120 people who were already part of Jesus' church gathered in the upper room waiting for the promise of the Holy Spirit's baptism. What we do see about these apostles is that they represent this new church. In Revelation 21, we see them representing all of the churches throughout all ages in the foundations of the New Jerusalem.

Throughout the three and half years of Jesus' ministry, He directs His Jewish church. This body, that He has called out, was still under the authority of the law covenant. He sent them out to make new converts, but they were instructed to go only to Israel. *Matthew 10:5-7 "These twelve Jesus sent forth, and commanded them, saying, Go not into the way of the Gentiles, and into any city of the Samaritans enter ye not: But go rather to the lost sheep of the house of Israel. And as ye go, preach, saying, The kingdom of heaven is at hand."* The authority to form Gentile churches did not come until after He had fulfilled the law covenant. *Colossians 2:14 "Blotting out the handwriting of ordinances that was against us, which was contrary to us, and took it out of the way, nailing it to his cross."*

Why take the time to document the passing of authority by God to His chosen people of the new covenant? It is important because we live in a time when religious people scoff at the need for a clear path of authority. For this reason, conclusions are made that put all of the saved in the bride of Christ. It produces teachings that tell us everyone will be the same in heaven. It is taught that everyone will receive every promise offered by God, that is, everyone receives crowns, everyone lives in the New Jerusalem, everyone walks on the streets of gold, and everybody will eat the fruit from the tree of life. It was very clear under the covenant made with Israel that God had specific rules of authority to receive His blessings. Very few biblical teachers will deny the total authority and control that God had with Israel. It seems some New Testament teachers struggle with this teaching of authority under the new covenant. It is a grace covenant but that does not exclude God's order upon His people.

Jesus left His church with the marching orders in Matthew 28. Their instructions for every age are outlined in this commission. These words were not to all the saved of all ages, but specifically to His visible church. After His resurrection and before His ascension back to heaven, He again instructs them concerning their future. *Acts 1:4-5 "And, being assembled together with them, commanded them that they should not depart from Jerusalem, but wait for the promise of the Father, which, saith he, ye have heard of me. For John truly baptized with water; but ye shall be baptized with the Holy Ghost not many days hence.* " He speaks to them about the baptism of the Holy Spirit, which will come on them as they obey Him and go to the upper room : *Acts 1:8, "But ye shall receive power, after that the Holy Ghost is come upon you: and ye shall be witnesses unto me both in Jerusalem, and in all Judaea, and in Samaria, and unto the uttermost part of the earth.* " This is His extended commission to them. They are to go worldwide producing new churches. They are to preach the gospel to all. To those who are saved, they are to instruct them about their need for baptism and service in the church that Jesus built.

The church began to grow in Jerusalem and it became huge in size as compared to most churches of our times. In Acts 2:41, 3,000 people were saved. In Acts 4:4, 5,000 men were saved, this number does not include the number of women and children who were saved. The number of the men was given to show the amount of families that were coming into this new church. In Acts 2:47, we are told that God was adding to the church daily such as should be saved. Some have estimated the size of the Jerusalem church to be close to 50,000. However, the members of the Jerusalem church were not following God's instructions to go into the whole world and grow His church. Because they were not obeying God, He allowed persecution to come upon this first church and they were scattered. Groups of them would end up in other cities and countries where new churches began. When the persecution started in the Jerusalem church, it became necessary to flee to other areas. It was understood that these saved, baptized, Holy Spirit-filled members would do the work that God had given them the authority to do. A church was started in Antioch in Syria, and they were led by the Lord to do missionary work. No doubt, this same thing was happening with other churches that had come out of the Jerusalem church.

> Now there were in the church that was at Antioch certain prophets and teachers; as Barnabas, and Simeon that was called Niger, and Lucius of Cyrene, and Manaen, which had been brought up with Herod the tetrarch, and Saul. As they ministered to the Lord, and fasted, the Holy Ghost said, Separate me Barnabas and Saul for the work whereunto I have called them. And when they had fasted and prayed, and laid their hands on them, they sent them away. So they, being sent forth by the Holy Ghost, departed unto Seleucia; and from thence they sailed to Cyprus. (Acts 13:1-4)

This scripture tells us there were five men working in the Antioch church as teachers, or prophets: Barnabas, Simeon, Lucius, Manaen, and Saul (Paul). While the church was fasting and praying, the Holy Spirit said to the Antioch church, "I have a work that I want Paul and Barnabas to do, separate them for the work I have called them to." The church then laid hands on them (ordained them) and sent them to do the work the Holy Spirit directed them to do.

We notice two things about these scriptures as they relate to authority in church planting (missionary work). One, the Holy Spirit placed it on the hearts of Paul and Barnabas to go to this destination. Two, He laid it on the church's heart to send them. God does not by-pass His eternal purposes. Just as Jesus would not by-pass the authority of John's baptism, the Holy Spirit will not by-pass the authority of the church. God's vehicle for missionary work is the church. Why in the world would the Holy Spirit waste His time telling the church to separate and send them if the church has no authority?

Paul and Barnabas were sent by the authority of the Antioch church to follow the leadership of the Holy Spirit and start churches. On this journey, as well as the two that followed, the Antioch church did not tell them where they should go. The Holy Spirit was doing the directing. He led them to people who needed a church to serve the Lord. Even though the Holy Spirit was directing them He did not direct them to go anywhere until He prompted the Antioch church to send them.

Again, God does not lead people to serve Him outside of the churches that have His authority, just like Jesus would not allow anyone to baptize Him but the man with the authority. It is suggested that the three missionary journeys of Paul produced about 20 churches. Other churches were sending men out to start churches and history reveals that great numbers were established as the passing of authority from church to church continued in the first century. God's promise that the "gates of hell" would not stop His church has continued to this very hour. His promise was that He would never leave this church. Ephesians 3:21 tells us, He would get glory through this church in every age.

On the day of Pentecost, the Holy Spirit baptized the church. It was a promise Jesus had made to His church. This baptism was not on individuals per-say, but on the entire body of Christ, the church. The passing of that power, which began in Jerusalem has been done through church planting. It has continued from Pentecost until today. The baptism of the Holy Spirit happened one time when the church of Jerusalem had the Holy Spirit come upon them. That indwelling of the Spirit has been passed on to the new churches birthed by the authority of the true churches with a lineage back to Jerusalem.

There are groups of people today who claim that individuals can get this baptism. Some of them even claim that one must receive this baptism to confirm their salvation. When scriptures are examined in context, it becomes clear that the baptism of the Holy Spirit was a promise made by Jesus to His church while He ministered with them. He informed them that the gift of the Holy Spirit was going to be given to them after His return to heaven. There were 120 members of Jesus' church assembled in the upper room when the "promise" came on the church,

Acts 2:1-4.

God's mission plan has been going on in every age. When we look at the dark times in our history when a false church connected to the state government had the power to kill those who disagreed with them,; we see the " gates of hell" trying to prevail against God's faithful, true to His Word, churches. The faithful witness of these churches could not be hidden, and we are still able to see the unbroken chain of churches prevailing. The chain of God's authority is still rattling today and true churches can be found all over the globe.

Twenty-Five
The High Cost

As we have viewed the *Great* city and the surrounding landscape of the eternal ages, it has become abundantly well-defined that God has a "prize" for His faithful children. The revelation of God concerning this "high calling," has uncovered a majestic, glorious, and unbridled grandeur that only the sovereign God of the universe could afford! His offer to sin-cursed humanity of the opportunity to not only become the very children of God but then be given the proposal of marriage to His Son overwhelms our minds.

When we were born into God's family and indwelt with the Holy Spirit of God, we became a new creation in Christ Jesus. The joy, peace, and satisfaction that we felt that day were as nothing we had ever experienced! Most of us would say that day was so amazing that we would have been willing to die and leave for heaven immediately. To consider that our heavenly Father had even bigger and better things in store for us wouldn't have seemed possible!

Peter, an apostle of Jesus Christ, to the strangers scattered
throughout Pontus, Galatia, Cappadocia, Asia, and

Bithynia, Elect according to the foreknowledge of God the Father, through sanctification of the Spirit, unto obedience and sprinkling of the blood of Jesus Christ: Grace unto you, and peace, be multiplied. Blessed be the God and Father of our Lord Jesus Christ, which according to his abundant mercy hath begotten us again unto a lively hope by the resurrection of Jesus Christ from the dead, (1 Peter 1:1-3)

On God's part, the cost of our birth into His family has been very high! *1 Peter 1:18-19, "Forasmuch as ye know that ye were not redeemed with corruptible things, as silver and gold, from your vain conversation received by tradition from your fathers; But with the precious blood of Christ, as of a lamb without blemish and without spot:"* Not only was there a high cost paid for our redemption from hell but there was also a high cost for the church in which He provided His children a place to love and serve Him. *Acts 20:28, "Take heed therefore unto yourselves, and to all the flock, over the which the Holy Ghost hath made you overseers, to feed the church of God, which he hath purchased with his own blood."*

In this present age, there are mixed opinions concerning the expectations God has for His children. It is often heard of religious leaders and teachers that to demand a full commitment in service to God will put us back under the law. They proclaim that living under this new "grace covenant" releases us from obligations to give ourselves sacrificially unto the Lord. While it is true that we are no longer under the law covenant with its severe penalties, the new "grace covenant" still demands that we love the Lord with all of our mind, soul, and body. Jesus in Matthew 22:37 quotes from Deuteronomy 6:5 clearly showing that the need for faithful commitment applied under the Law as well as under grace.

The inspired Word of God doesn't leave us without multiple Scriptures that clearly state God's desire of a complete surrender of our lives to Him :

I beseech you therefore, brethren, by the mercies of God, that ye present your bodies a living sacrifice, holy, acceptable unto God, which is your reasonable service. And be not conformed to this world: but be ye transformed by the renewing of your mind, that ye may prove what is that good, and acceptable, and perfect, will of God. (Romans 12:1-2)

The Old Testament demanded animal sacrifices, which pictured what Messiah would do on the cross for the forgiveness of sin. Many violations of the law, given to Israel, demanded physical death. Under the grace covenant, God demands obedience to baptism, which pictures a burial of our old lives and death to sin.

We are charged by God to preach His Word that sets the pattern of sanctification or separation from sin. Not only are we commanded to come out from among the world we are also instructed to walk in righteousness. Sometimes, in the religious world we see teachings that encourage God's children that "grace" means we are not obligated to strictly follow God's commandments:

> I charge thee therefore before God, and the Lord Jesus Christ, who shall judge the quick and the dead at his appearing and his kingdom; Preach the word; be instant in season, out of season; reprove, rebuke, exhort with all longsuffering and doctrine. For the time will come when they will not endure sound doctrine; but after their own lusts shall they heap to themselves teachers, having itching ears; And they shall turn away their ears from the truth, and shall be turned unto fables. (2 Timothy 4:1-4)

Understanding that Jesus provided a church for His children to serve Him in is essential to conforming to His image. To be saved and not baptized is a violation of God's order and authority over Christian living. Being baptized has nothing to do with being born again, (saved.) It does, however, have everything to do with acknowledging our heavenly Father's authority over our lives. *1 Corinthians 6:19-20, "What? know ye not that your body is the temple of the Holy Ghost which is in you, which ye have of God, and ye are not your own? For ye are bought with a price: therefore glorify God in your body, and in your spirit, which are God's."* Yes, we were bought with a price; it cost God everything to birth us into His family. Therefore, because we are His children, He has expectations of us. *Ephesians 2:10, "For we are his workmanship, created in Christ Jesus unto good works, which God hath before ordained that we should walk in them."*

I trust that we would all want to be a part of that glorious bride and live in that special mansion that Jesus is preparing for His wife. He is not engaged to all the saved but only to the church He founded during His earthly ministry. It is only to this church that He gave the commission of Matthew 28:18-20. The authority to preach the gospel, baptize, and to teach people to observe all of His commandments was given to His church. This is why it is so important to be a member of a church that is remaining true to all of His teachings. *Jude 1:3, "Beloved, when I gave all diligence to write unto you of the common salvation, it was needful for me to write unto you, and exhort you that ye should earnestly contend for the faith which was once delivered unto the saints."* Not only has it been the duty of the Lord's church to keep and contend for the truth, she has been the vehicle that God has used in every age to be the source of truth. *1 Timothy 3:15, "But if I tarry long, that thou mayest know how thou oughtest to behave thyself in the house of God, which is the church of the living God, the pillar and ground of the truth."*

Many will teach that it is not necessary to serve God in a local, visible, church. They will say if we have been born again, we have full authority to serve God as independent contractors. Jesus did not spend three years on this earth calling out, teaching, and commissioning a church for us to disallow it by our own preferences. *Ephesians*

3:19-21, "And to know the love of Christ, which passeth knowledge, that ye might be filled with all the fulness of God. Now unto him that is able to do exceeding abundantly above all that we ask or think, according to the power that worketh in us, Unto him be glory in the church by Christ Jesus throughout all ages, world without end. Amen."

How much faithfulness is required to be a part of the bride of Christ? We will ask another question before we answer this one. When a man and a woman commit to each other in marriage, How faithful do they have to be, if they want the marriage to transpire? Earthly engagements are for examining how strong their love is. They must be exclusive to each other.

Consider this scenario, a man is engaged to a woman and they determine a time for a date. The day of the date, a friend asks him to go fishing, if he accepts, he will not be able to go out with his fiancée. Would this be a problem? Later, he is out of town on business and his fiancée is asked by a man at work to go out for dinner. If she accepts would this be a problem? When he returns, they are at the mall, and he meets some people from his job—he doesn't introduce her and then has a conversation acting like she isn't even there. Does this seem problematic? The next evening, they go out for dinner: she dresses in scanty clothing and winks at other men in the restaurant. Could this injure their relationship? How much faithfulness is required?

Being engaged to Jesus as His espoused bride should mean that we are exclusive to each other. As in our scenario above, we make a commitment to serve Him faithfully in His church. But suppose on Saturday night a friend calls and asks if we would like to meet him at the lake for a day of fishing on his new bass boat. If this is not enough, he tells us he is bringing his barbecue grill and has some T-bone steaks and his wife has made her famous potato salad. "Bring the wife and kids we will have a great time." Surely, Jesus will understand if we miss church services, we don't get offers like this every day! How much faithfulness is required?

Some would probably argue that we shouldn't be expected to be involved in all of the services of the church. Others might contend that if an employer demanded our services we would have no choice. With our human reasoning, we will find many reasons for not obeying God's word. *Hebrews 10:25-26, "Not forsaking the assembling of ourselves together, as the manner of some is; but exhorting one another: and so much the more, as ye see the day approaching. For if we sin wilfully after that we have received the knowledge of the truth, there remaineth no more sacrifice for sins,"* I have often heard that God understands, He knows sometimes, we just don't have any choice.

Let's look at a few scriptures and see if we can't get a better perspective of God's desires for us! *Luke 14:26-2, "If any man come to me, and hate not his father, and mother, and wife, and children, and brethren, and sisters, yea, and his own life also, he cannot be my disciple. And whosoever doth not bear his cross, and come after me, cannot be my disciple."* Wow! This is a hard saying, who can hear it?

This verse is not telling us that we need to loathe or detest our families; it is telling us that Jesus has to be first.

When God reveals what a man who will marry a wife must do. He says, *Matthew 19:5, "And said, For this cause shall a man leave father and mother, and shall cleave to his wife: and they twain shall be one flesh?"* Again, God is not telling married couples they have to abandon their families. He tells us our lives and priorities change when we marry. We are no longer under our parent's authority. The husband and wife must "cleave" unto each other. Jesus expects the same of His children who have been obedient to baptism and have entered into engagement with Him by joining the body He is engaged to. That body is His church and if we are part of it the responsibility of engagement is upon us because He is always faithful.

To some, putting ourselves in a place where there are restrictions or expectations would be too much to ask. The real issue is whether we are in love with Jesus:

> He that hath my commandments, and keepeth them, he it is that loveth me: and he that loveth me shall be loved of my Father, and I will love him, and will manifest myself to him. Judas saith unto him, not Iscariot, Lord, how is it that thou wilt manifest thyself unto us, and not unto the world? Jesus answered and said unto him, If a man love me, he will keep my words: and my Father will love him, and we will come unto him, and make our abode

with him. He that loveth me not keepeth not my sayings: and the word which ye hear is not mine, but the Father's which sent me. (John 14:21-24)

Jesus offers full freedom to those who love Him. Our time becomes His time, and like the newly engaged couple, we just can't get enough of each other. *John 8:36, "If the Son therefore shall make you free, ye shall be free indeed."*

Our fleshly nature rebels against being told what to do. We want to do our own thing and not allow anyone else to control us. *Galatians 5:17, "For the flesh lusteth against the Spirit, and the Spirit against the flesh: and these are contrary the one to the other: so that ye cannot do the things that ye would."* Many of God's children still walk in their fleshly nature. They say; "I don't want to be a member of a church and be expected to be in every service. I don't want to feel obligated to tithe and give offerings. I am the master of my own ship." *1 John 5:2-3, "By this we know that we love the children of God, when we love God, and keep his commandments. For this is the love of God, that we keep his commandments: and his commandments are not grievous."* The whole issue of serving God is attitude based. If we approach it as a duty and not because we are love motivated, it will become "grievous."

It is imperative that we understand the answer to this question "How much faithfulness is required to be a part of the bride of Christ?" God's Word has much to say on this subject. We will continue to examine the requirements in the next chapter. *2 John 1:6, "And this is love, that we walk after his commandments. This is the commandment, That, as ye have heard from the beginning, ye should walk in it."*

Twenty-Six
High Expectations

Does God expect righteous living from those who will marry His Son? Does Jesus desire a wife who has proven herself faithful during the engagement? I have heard a statement from people who struggle with being part of a church. Here is the conclusion, "They just expect too much from their members!" This might have been said because the pastor had presented a message about what the Bible says about financial giving. Maybe, it concerned a sin that was presented as unChristian and one that they practiced. They didn't feel that it was anybody's business but their own how they lived their lives. The idea of someone having control over their lives was offensive to them.

Thoughts like these are not uncommon in the world we live in. Because we are sinners by nature, we often choose to live by our own standards. *Isaiah 55:9, "For as the heavens are higher than the earth, so are my ways higher than your ways, and my thoughts than your thoughts."* It is not unusual to hear the statement; "It is my body, I will do with it what I want."

When we see a man and a woman announce that they have

entered into an engagement, we assume they have become exclusive to each other. If we hear the woman or the man say something like; "It's my life, he/she is not going to tell me how to live," we roll our eyes and say, "Oh, Oh!" We are pretty sure the marriage will not take place if their attitude doesn't change. Why would we conclude that Jesus is going to marry a people who have not proven how much they love Him by the pledge of their lives?

The Bible clearly reveals Jesus is only engaged to His church and only those who are part of the church will be a part of the bride. Because of this, some conclude that having their name on a church role will guarantee them a place in the holy city. This couldn't be further from the truth. The bride Jesus marries will be without spot and blemish. *Ephesians 5:25-27, "Husbands, love your wives, even as Christ also loved the church, and gave himself for it; That he might sanctify and cleanse it with the washing of water by the word, That he might present it to himself a glorious church, not having spot, or wrinkle, or any such thing; but that it should be holy and without blemish."*

Why must the standards of Christian living be so *high* in the Lord's church? Think back to these scriptures:

> *And he that sat was to look upon like a jasper and a sardine stone: and there was a rainbow round about the throne, in sight like unto an emerald. And round about the throne were four and twenty seats: and upon the*

seats I saw four and twenty elders sitting, clothed in white raiment; and they had on their heads crowns of gold. And out of the throne proceeded lightnings and thunderings and voices: and there were seven lamps of fire burning before the throne, which are the seven Spirits of God. And before the throne there was a sea of glass like unto crystal: and in the midst of the throne, and round about the throne, were four beasts full of eyes before and behind. And the first beast was like a lion, and the second beast like a calf, and the third beast had a face as a man, and the fourth beast was like a flying eagle. And the four beasts had each of them six wings about him; and they were full of eyes within: and they rest not day and night, saying, Holy, holy, holy, Lord God Almighty, which was, and is, and is to come. And when those beasts give glory and honour and thanks to him that sat on the throne, who liveth for ever and ever, The four and twenty elders fall down before him that sat on the throne, and worship him that liveth for ever and ever, and cast their crowns before the throne, saying, Thou art worthy, O Lord, to receive glory and honour and power: for thou hast created all things, and for thy pleasure they are and were created. (Revelation 4:3-11)

Seeing Jesus sitting on His throne in all of His glory and perfection reveals something about the bride that will sit with Him. This is Jesus sitting on this throne. Read verse 8 again, *"And the four beasts had each of them six wings about him; and they were full of eyes within: and they rest not day and night, saying, Holy, holy, holy, Lord God Almighty,* **which was, and is, and is to come.** *"* Without question, He is the One to come. He is coming with His bride and they will rule and reign throughout eternity.

Can you feel the purity of this scene in heaven? We view the angels and special creatures that are worshiping the God of the eternal ages. What a picture, pure worship emanating from everyone present. The 24 elders are casting crowns before the feet of Jesus. The full manifestation of the Holy Spirit of God is exalting the One without sin. What are they all proclaiming? *Holy ! Holy! Holy!* to God who is Lord with all power! Nothing can stand in His presence that is unholy! When we view this scene in heaven, a great truth leaps out at us. Only ignorance could make us think that joining the Lord's church and getting our names on the role would include us in the bride that will sit with the bridegroom on His throne!

Often, people who have become members of a church ask questions about how faithful they have to be. Do I have to attend every service at my church? Is it ok to have a glass of wine with my meals? Do I have to read my Bible every day? If I am at a restaurant, do I need to pray and thank God for the meal? Does God expect me to teach the gospel to my friends and relatives? If someone has hurt my feelings, do I have to forgive them even if they do not ask for it? The list could go on for many pages and chapters but the answer to these and similar questions can be found in *2 Timothy 2:15, "Study to shew thyself approved unto God, a workman that needeth not to be ashamed, rightly dividing the word of truth."* Who do we want to be pleased with our conduct,? Is it a pastor, fellow church member, or the people of our community? The answer is, "approved by God!" We love Jesus and we want Him to be pleased with us. He is the one we are engaged to, and we want Him to be excited about our love for Him.

2 Timothy 2:11-12, "It is a faithful saying: For if we be dead with him, we shall also live with him: If we suffer, we shall also reign with him: if we deny him, he also will deny us:" "If we be dead to sin," is the qualifier, not if we get our names on the church role. If we suffer and take up our cross, following Jesus that we might be conformed to His image, is how we will make ourselves ready for the marriage.

Baptism is essential to becoming a member of a true church but it's not just a ceremony that gets us into a church.

> *What shall we say then? Shall we continue in sin, that grace may abound? God forbid. How shall we, that are dead to sin, live any longer therein? Know ye not, that so many of us as were baptized into Jesus Christ were baptized into his death? Therefore we are buried with him by baptism into death: that like as Christ was raised up from the dead by the glory of the Father, even so we*

also should walk in newness of life. (Romans 6:1-4)

After we are born into God's family, our first step of obedience is to be baptized and added to the church. This act is a declaration that the blood of Jesus Christ separated us from the sin that condemned us to an eternity in hell. It further proclaims a commitment on our part to bury our old lives of sin. We vow to walk in a new way, excluding sin from our lives and replacing it with righteousness. The question was asked of the members of the church in Rome:; "How can we continue to live in sin, knowing that when we were baptized we publicly stated that we would become dead to our old sinful lifestyles?

The expectation of God for our lives is plainly stated here again in *Romans 6:12-13, "Let not sin therefore reign in your mortal body, that ye should obey it in the lusts thereof. Neither yield ye your members as instruments of unrighteousness unto sin: but yield yourselves unto God, as those that are alive from the dead, and your members as instruments of righteousness unto God."* What would make any believer in Christ think God is okay with us doing our own thing? It would seem that failing to study God's Word might be the source of this attitude. When Jesus prayed for His church and their well-being after His departure, He said this, *John 17:15-17, "I pray not that thou shouldest take them out of the world, but that thou shouldest keep them from the evil. They are not of the world, even as I am not of the world. Sanctify them through thy truth: thy word is truth."* The sanctification of our lives can only come to us as we study God's Word and let its truth direct our paths. *Psalms 119:11, "Thy word have I hid in mine heart, that I might not sin against thee."*

Do scriptures that talk about our *freedom* in Christ give us an excuse for not following His commands? In the Commission to the church in Matthew 28, Jesus said, we are to be *"Teaching them to observe all things whatsoever I have commanded you:"* The operative words being, "to observe." It is not enough for us to teach doctrines that give clear paths to righteous living, we must emphasize that putting these truths into practice is essential. When we are questioned why we need to attend church regularly, or why we must study our Bibles, it might be time for a lesson on *love* and the benefits of engagement. We do not stop participating in the sins of the world, i.e. zero-tolerance for illegal drugs, alcohol, tobacco, adultery, fornication, pornography, lying, cheating, stealing, etc. because the church told us we have to. We stop because we love Jesus and those things offend Him. When Christ talks about making us **free indeed**, He is revealing a way of life that removes the restrictiveness of sin. This, of course, begins at the point of the new birth when the condemnation of hell is removed. It doesn't stop here because each step we take in the process of sanctification further removes us from the power of sin over our lives.

God does not save us and then leave us without a plan that will guide us through life!

Nevertheless the foundation of God standeth sure, having this seal, The Lord knoweth them that are his. And, Let every one that nameth the name of Christ depart from iniquity. But in a great house there are not only vessels of gold and of silver, but also of wood and of earth; and some to honour, and some to dishonour. If a man therefore purge himself from these, he shall be a vessel unto honour, sanctified, and meet for the master's use, and prepared unto every good work. (2 Timothy 2:19-21)

His desire is to keep His children from the depressive power of sin. *1 Thessalonians 5:22-24, "Abstain from all appearance of evil. And the very God of peace sanctify you wholly; and I pray God your whole spirit and soul and body be preserved blameless unto the coming of our Lord Jesus Christ. Faithful is he that calleth you, who also will do it."* We must strive to make our calling and election sure.

Twenty-Seven
The Dilemma

There is a song from the past that says, "Everybody wants to go to heaven, but nobody wants to die." Viewing the bride and the New Jerusalem, as we have in the previous chapters, has set a "prize" before us. This should spark a desire in all of us. Even so, it seems like the sentiments of the song might apply to the bride of Christ as well. Most would like to be a part of it but many are not willing to meet the qualifications. I want to be one of those in the bride! I want to live in the new city and walk on those streets of gold. Most of all I want to live where Jesus lives with His bride. I don't believe I'm alone in this desire. The opportunity is too great to dismiss it without considering what God is offering. We, who are born again, have the Holy Spirit living in us. The spiritual side of us should give us a desire like Paul, to "press toward the mark for the prize of the high calling of God in Christ Jesus."

This being true, why do we see so much "passive" Christianity in our world? Why don't we see more of God's children excited about leaving this world and being with Jesus? Listen to the passion of the apostle as he thinks of heaven. *Philippians 1:23, "For I am in a strait betwixt two, having a desire to depart, and to be with Christ; which is far better."* Could it be, that instead of being "pilgrims" passing through this life, we have become "settlers"? We have our comfortable homes, nice vehicles, challenging employment, wonderful children, joyous grandchildren, recreational vehicles and toys, and many just don't want to leave it all behind. When we hear preaching and teaching about the "soon" return of Jesus, are we thrilled like John? *Revelation 22:20, "He which testifieth these things saith, Surely I come quickly. Amen. Even so, come, Lord Jesus."*

Have you ever thought? "If only I had lost my human nature the day I was saved, it would be so much easier!" Daily we are tempted to follow our fleshly desires. Jesus knew we would struggle with the flesh so He instructs us in *Matthew 26:41, "Watch and pray, that ye enter not into temptation: the spirit indeed is willing, but the flesh is weak."* Have you ever wondered why God left us in these sinful bodies after He saved us? He knew the flesh would be weak but He also knew that it would be the source of advantage for us to reveal our **love** to Jesus. Paul, by inspiration, unfolds the problem:

> *I find then a law, that, when I would do good, evil is present with me. For I delight in the law of God after the inward man: But I see another law in my members, warring against the law of my mind, and bringing me into captivity to the law of sin which is in my members. O*

wretched man that I am! who shall deliver me from the body of this death? I thank God through Jesus Christ our Lord. So then with the mind I myself serve the law of God; but with the flesh the law of sin. (Romans 7:21-25)

It will cost us to live the dedicated sanctified life. Are we willing to pay the cost that will result in us living with Jesus as His bride? It is a dilemma because even though many saved people would like to be in the bride, they are not willing to pay the cost. The high aim of being Jesus' chosen bride can only be achieved by walking in the Spirit. Paul understood, from personal experience, the problems associated with choosing the straight and narrow path. It is easy for the preacher or teacher to present the simplicity of "walking in the Spirit," it is quite another thing to do it. Even the teacher and preacher will be subject to the human nature. *Romans 7:18-19, "For I know that in me (that is, in my flesh,) dwelleth no good thing: for to will is present with me; but how to perform that which is good I find not. For the good that I would I do not: but the evil which I would not, that I do."* God inspired Paul to write about his dilemma because He wanted us to see that we are not the only ones facing this issue.

I want to be in the bride of Christ. I know that Jesus is only engaged to His church; therefore, I must have the baptism that is acceptable to God and membership in this church. I also know that just having my name on the church role will not guarantee me entrance into the bride. What should you do? Yes, this is the dilemma. But praise the Lord, He has not left us in the dark about the solution to making the "mark." The book of Galatians presents the issue and sets the path to achieving this "high calling."

> This I say then, Walk in the Spirit, and ye shall not fulfil the lust of the flesh. For the flesh lusteth against the Spirit, and the Spirit against the flesh: and these are contrary the one to the other: so that ye cannot do the things that ye would. But if ye be led of the Spirit, ye are not under the law. Now the works of the flesh are manifest, which are these; Adultery, fornication, uncleanness, lasciviousness, Idolatry, witchcraft, hatred, variance, emulations, wrath, strife, seditions, heresies, Envyings, murders, drunkenness, revellings, and such like: of the which I tell you before, as I have also told you in time past, that they which do such things shall not inherit the kingdom of God. But the fruit of the Spirit is love, joy, peace, longsuffering, gentleness, goodness, faith, Meekness, temperance: against such there is no law. And they that are Christ's have crucified the flesh with the affections and lusts. If we live in the Spirit, let us also walk in the Spirit. Let us not be desirous of vain glory, provoking one another, envying one another. (Galatians 5:16-26)

These are great scriptures that give us the plan for success in overcoming sin in our human bodies. No matter how messed up our lives might be, here is that "magic pill" that gives answers on how to overcome sin.

I say "magic pill" with tongue in cheek. When doing biblical counseling, I find most people come thinking there is a simple pill that will fix their problems. Actually, the Bible does have simple answers for overcoming sin but not everyone is willing to follow God's plan. These scriptures in Galatians are rich with information that we need if we are to be successful in our desire to live with Jesus in the place He has prepared for His bride.

"This I say then, Walk in the Spirit, and ye shall not fulfil the lust of the flesh. For the flesh lusteth against the Spirit, and the Spirit against the flesh: and these are contrary the one to the other: so that ye cannot do the things that ye would." Walking in the Spirit is key to our victory! The person we were before we received Christ as our Savior changed the very moment the Holy Spirit birthed us. The physical birth received from our earthly parents, had only given us a nature that was contrary to God. *Romans 8:7-8, "Because the carnal mind is enmity against God: for it is not subject to the law of God, neither indeed can be. So then they that are in the flesh cannot please God."*

Before we trusted Jesus for salvation, we had no capacity to "walk in the Spirit." When we were born into God's family, we became a new creation with new powers from God. *1 Corinthians 6:19-20,*

"What? know ye not that your body is the temple of the Holy Ghost which is in you, which ye have of God, and ye are not your own? For ye are bought with a price: therefore glorify God in your body, and in your spirit, which are God's." These scriptures in Galatians give us hope that it is possible to live godly in this present world. We do not have to muster up strength on our own to figure out how to walk in the Spirit. The indwelling Spirit will be our guide.

Continuing with these scriptures from Galatians 5, we find information about the things that will keep us from being in Christ's bride.

> Now the works of the flesh are manifest, which are these; Adultery, fornication, uncleanness, lasciviousness, Idolatry, witchcraft, hatred, variance, emulations, wrath, strife, seditions, heresies, Envyings, murders, drunkenness, revellings, and such like: of the which I tell you before, as I have also told you in time past, that they which do such things shall not inherit the kingdom of God. Galatians (5:19-21)

The Bible is not a catalog of sins, yet God wants us to know about the things that He will not tolerate. We know God hates sin. *Psalms 45:6-7, "Thy throne, O God, is for ever and ever: the sceptre of thy kingdom is a right sceptre. Thou lovest righteousness, and hatest wickedness: therefore God, thy God, hath anointed thee with the oil of gladness above thy fellows."* Galatians, verse 21 says, *"... that they which do such things shall not inherit the kingdom of God."* Keep in mind he is not talking to unregenerate people, nor is He indicating the possibility of lost salvation. He is talking to the saved, baptized, members of the church at Galatia. Christ and His bride will rule the eternal kingdom. The disobedient children will not be part of the eternal government. All of the sins mentioned in these scriptures are sins saved people commit. Sadly, too many of God's children violate these offenses on a regular basis.

I said this list is not the catalog of all sins, but it is a list of general sins that any specific sin could fit in. As a pastor of a church for many years, I have often been asked if a specific action was a sin. "Pastor, is smoking marijuana a sin? I don't find it mentioned anywhere in the Bible. What is wrong with smoking cigarettes or drinking a beer?" Because God knew sinful man would want to try new sins out if they found a catalog that listed every sin, He just left us a general list. For His children He not only left this list, He placed the Holy Spirit in our hearts to convict of things that are wrong:

> *Nevertheless I tell you the truth; It is expedient for you that I go away: for if I go not away, the Comforter will not come unto you; but if I depart, I will send him unto you. And when he is come, he will reprove the world of sin, and of righteousness, and of judgment: Of sin, because they believe not on me; Of righteousness, because I go to my Father, and ye see me no more; Of judgment, because*

the prince of this world is judged. (John 16:7-11)

These Scriptures are definitely a dilemma to those who want to believe they will be in the bride just because they have their name on the church role. This list of sins makes it clear that they which do such things, will not be included in the bride of Christ. Thus, it is righteous living, along with membership in the body that Jesus is engaged to that qualifies one for this relationship. The good news is, that if one is doing any of these sins, they can confess, and repent and be restored. *1 John 1:9, "If we confess our sins, he is faithful and just to forgive us our sins, and to cleanse us from all unrighteousness."*

Finally, we examine what walking in the Spirit will produce. *"But the fruit of the Spirit is love, joy, peace, longsuffering, gentleness, goodness, faith, Meekness, temperance: against such there is no law. And they that are Christ's have crucified the flesh with the affections and lusts. If we live in the Spirit, let us also walk in the Spirit"* (Galatians 5:22-23). Wow! Living and walking in the Spirit promises us the highest quality of life here on this earth, as well as out in eternity.

These Scriptures are what set the recipients of the bride apart from the nominal believer. I am always surprised when doing biblical counseling and a person comes describing himself or herself as a defeated Christian. Often, they reveal that they are feeling totally unspiritual. Sometimes, it is because their marriage isn't working and this is affecting their Christian walk. The reasons why they are not excited about serving God are multiple. Why am I surprised? Because God has the remedy for all of our problems! If we want to be prepared for the marriage of the Lamb, we must stay in control of our Christian walk. God has simple answers for how to serve Him and love doing it. He has answers for everything that pertains to life and godliness in His Word. These Scriptures in Galatians 5 are so profound in guiding us to the means of solving the issues that keep us from successful Christian living.

Here is a question I often ask in counseling, "Could you be filled with love, joy, peace, longsuffering, gentleness, goodness, faith, and meekness and still have your problems?" Of course, the answer is an emphatic no! Often when that person is questioned about their walk in the Spirit, they come up short. They are not attending church faithfully and not reading their Bibles daily. When questioned about their prayer life it is found deficient. They may be praying about their issue, but they are not able to get past the, "It's all about me" syndrome. Walking in the Spirit involves stepping out of the flesh.

Furthermore, we have to understand the difference between walking in the Spirit and walking in the flesh. *"For the flesh lusteth against the Spirit, and the Spirit against the flesh: and these are contrary the one to the other: so that ye cannot do the things that ye would."* To walk in the Spirit we must stop walking in the flesh. For our problem to depart, we must first discover the sins causing it. Once we deal with the sin, something amazing happens. We step out of the flesh and find ourselves walking in the Spirit. The absence of sin in the Christian's life begins a natural progression of the spiritual walk. The fruits start manifesting themselves. Love, joy, peace, etc. take control of our lives. What causes these fruits to stop manifesting themselves is a return to walking in the flesh. Because we are sinners by nature, the dilemma is the need for a daily cleansing of sin to keep us out of the flesh walk.

Sometimes, it is hard to have the faith to believe that leaving the sin behind is easy. God is faithful and just to forgive us our sins when we confess them to Him. Usually, the counselee doesn't want to admit the sins that are causing his or her problems. It might be an overeating sin. It might be a job-related sin; lying, cheating, deception. Sometimes it is a sexual sin, involvement in adultery, fornication, homosexuality, or pornography. It might be caused because of addictive behavior that they know is not pleasing to God, i.e. cigarettes, alcohol, drug abuse, illegal and even prescription drugs. Sometimes, it is caused by attitudinal behaviors such as anger, meanness, and physical abuse. The list could go on, but it has been my experience that when people forsake the sins of the flesh and nurture spiritual things, the walk in the Spirit blossoms. *Ezekiel 36:26-27, "A new heart also will I give you, and a new spirit will I put within you: and I will take away the stony heart out of your flesh, and I will give you an heart of flesh. And I will put my spirit within you, and cause you to walk in my statutes, and ye shall keep my judgments, and do them."*

Walking in the Spirit is not all about making us feel good. Galatians the fifth chapter reveals our need to love others. The first fruit mentioned is love, and it is necessary before any of the other fruits develop. *Galatians 5:13-14, "For, brethren, ye have been called unto liberty; only use not liberty for an occasion to the flesh, but by love serve one another. For all the law is fulfilled in one word, even in this; Thou shalt love thy neighbour as thyself."* Seeking to love our neighbor first removes us from our self-loving behavior. Our neighbor could be someone who lives in our own home. It could be a spouse, our children, or a relative. Getting burdened about sharing the gospel with the lost will change our focus on life. It will also change our attitudes. There are people who need God in their lives everywhere. We will not run out of opportunities to share the gospel. Our lives will change when we start walking in the Spirit and loving those around us. The product of this love is a new life that becomes profitable for our Savior. The rest of the fruits start to come alive as we let love for others direct our paths. We'll start enjoying the experience of joy and peace. The next thing we know, we have become patient and longsuffering with those around us.

In conclusion, these scriptures are our guides to meeting the qualifications that will make us ready for the marriage of the Lamb! No greater opportunity has been set before the children of God than that of being married to God's Son.

Twenty-Eight
Journey Through Time

Jesus called out His bride during His earthly ministry. As we have seen in previous chapters, God's man with authority, John the Baptist, fulfilled his calling to "make ready a people prepared for the Lord" (Luke 1:17). Furthermore, we discovered Jesus walking a great distance to begin His ministry by receiving John's baptism. Jesus then called out His church on the seashore of Galilee. These men were part of the material John had prepared for Him. Jesus then took this new church and by His authority as God, gave them the job of baptizing the new converts. (John 4:1, 2). Jesus taught this new church the doctrines that would sustain them throughout all time.

Jesus educated His church by teaching them that this church would outlive them. The promise wasn't that Jesus was going to preserve these men from the attacks of Satan as individuals but that the church they represented, was going to be preserved in every age. *Matthew 16:18, "And I say also unto thee, That thou art Peter, and upon this rock I will build my church; and the gates of hell shall not prevail against it."* All the powers of Satan's evil influence will never be able to stop her. Satan's government empowered church would never be able to kill or destroy enough of God's churches to make her go out of existence. At least fifty million people in the dark ages lost their lives standing for the doctrines delivered to the true church by her founder Jesus Christ. The doctrine of the perpetuity of the church is proven by the historical "trail of blood."

Furthermore, it is plain to see in the "Great Commission" given by Jesus to His church, that He would empower them throughout all ages:

> *And Jesus came and spake unto them, saying, All power is given unto me in heaven and in earth. Go ye therefore, and teach all nations, baptizing them in the name of the Father, and of the Son, and of the Holy Ghost: Teaching them to observe all things whatsoever I have commanded you: and, lo, I am with you alway, even unto the end of the world. Amen. (Matthew 28:18-20)*

Here, He spoke to His church about their job until He returns. These men were only going to live their short lives and then die. The promise wasn't to these men but to the body they comprised, His church. This commission is still in full force today being carried out by the faithful espoused bride of Jesus.

In the previous chapters, we saw that after the resurrection of Jesus, He met with this church in Acts 1, telling them to wait in the upper room. They were to remain there until they received the Holy

Spirit's baptism:

> To whom also he shewed himself alive after his passion by many infallible proofs, being seen of them forty days, and speaking of the things pertaining to the kingdom of God: And, being assembled together with them, commanded them that they should not depart from Jerusalem, but wait for the promise of the Father, which, saith he, ye have heard of me. For John truly baptized with water; but ye shall be baptized with the Holy Ghost not many days hence. (Acts 1:3-5)

After He told them of this baptism, He further extended the churches commission or marching orders. *Acts 1:8, "But ye shall receive power, after that the Holy Ghost is come upon you: and ye shall be witnesses unto me both in Jerusalem, and in all Judaea, and in Samaria, and unto the uttermost part of the earth."*

After being baptized by the Holy Spirit, they were given new powers and also some new direction. They were to establish churches in Judea and Samaria. Judea became the second church in the line of succession. Up until now, only the Jews were allowed to be in the Lord's church. This happened because until the payment on the cross, they were still bound by the law covenant. *Colossians 2:14, "Blotting out the handwriting of ordinances that was against us, which was contrary to us, and took it out of the way, nailing it to his cross"*

The next church in the chain of succession was the Samaritan church:

> *Then Philip went down to the city of Samaria, and preached*
> *Christ unto them. And the people with one accord gave*
> *heed unto those things which Philip spake, hearing and*
> *seeing the miracles which he did. For unclean spirits,*
> *crying with loud voice, came out of many that were*
> *possessed with them: and many taken with palsies, and*
> *that were lame, were healed. And there was great joy*
> *in that city. (Acts 8:5-8)*

The significance of the Samarian church was the Jewish members who were married to Gentiles; and they were considered unclean, as were the Gentiles. There doesn't seem to be much opposition to this from the pure Israelites. However, this was a major change in what the church had allowed up to this time.

The church now moved out to the "uttermost" parts of the earth, and Peter ended up in Caesarea at the house Cornelius. Cornelius, a Gentile centurion soldier had a dream telling him to send messengers to Peter in Joppa to tell him to come to his house. Meanwhile, back in Joppa, Peter had a dream where God showed him that he was not to consider Gentiles unclean any longer. When he awoke from his dream, the messengers from Cornelius had arrived, and Peter went to Caesarea to the house of Cornelius and . It was then that the first Gentile church was established. God allowed Cornelius and his family to have a similar demonstration of the power that came upon the Jerusalem church on the day of Pentecost. Peter then spoke to the other Jewish brethren and asked if any of them had a problem with these Gentiles being baptized and becoming a church. God used these spectacular events to make it clear that the door to His church has been opened to Gentiles.

God then called Paul to be the apostle to the Gentiles, *Acts 9:15-16, "But the Lord said unto him, Go thy way: for he is a chosen vessel unto me, to bear my name before the Gentiles, and kings, and the children of Israel: For I will shew him how great things he must suffer for my name's sake."* From this time forward, we find Paul laboring as an apostle to the Gentiles. He didn't stop loving the Jews and trying to win them to the Lord but his main focus became the establishment of Gentile churches.

Three long missionary journeys produced many Gentile churches and in turn, these Gentile churches began an outreach that stretches to the uttermost parts of the earth.

From the time that Zachariah was approached in the temple and told that he and Elizabeth would have a son, to the end of the apostolic age, there is a clear line of authority. This chain of authority began with John being sent to prepare the material for Jesus. Jesus, after receiving John's baptism, established His church from those John baptized. Jesus then gave His church authority to preach the gospel and to baptize those who will follow Him. This church, Jesus has called to be His bride, must always be cautious not to step out of the order of authority. The hand of God has sovereignly set the rules and the order of who will be the bride of His Son. The authority given to the Lord's church, to carry out His commission, continues even to this present time. The promise that the gates of hell will not prevail against her remains true to this day. The church has suffered devastating persecution in every age, but she has never compromised the doctrines Jesus left with her. In our next chapter, we begin to identify this church by the names she has been called.

Twenty-Nine
A Rose by Any Other Name

"A rose by any other name would smell as sweet" a frequently referenced part of William Shakespeare's play, *Romeo and Juliet*, where Juliet shares this thought with Romeo. As we near the end of this book, the identity of the bride becomes key to all we have examined thus far. Just as Juliet conveys to Romeo, it is not the name assigned to a rose that makes it a rose, the same will be seen true of Christ's bride.

The church organized, empowered, and engaged during the ministry of Christ was not given a name. Had Jesus said; "The name of my church shall be, Catholic, Methodist, Presbyterian, Lutheran, Pentecostal, Mormon, Jehovah Witness, Quakers, Anglican, Baptist, Mennonites, Church of Christ, Nondenominational, Assembly of God, or any other name, all groups that wanted to identify with Jesus would use that name. What was given was the authority to preach the good news that Jesus' death, burial, and resurrection would save lost sinners from hell and guarantee them eternal life in heaven. They were also given the authority to baptize those saved and bring them into the church. Once they became part of the body of Christ, they were instructed to teach the new ones to observe all of the things taught to them during His ministry here on earth.

These instructions would perpetuate to every age until the return of Jesus for His bride. His church did not end with the lives of these first members. These promises were to the church He built during His time on earth. He told them, Matthew, 28:20 *"Teaching them to observe all things whatsoever I have commanded you: and, lo, I am with you alway, even unto the end of the world. Amen."* After Jesus gave these *marching orders,* His church was obedient, following His commands and churches were established. All of these new churches were operating by the authority of these instructions. Even though there were many new churches established, they had one thing in common— they were connected through this chain of authority. The commission issued by Jesus bound these newly formed churches to the first church established by Him. They were each independent bodies, yet, connected by the same doctrines and teachings given by their Lord and founder. Every new church established could prove their linkage back to the "first church" by an examination of their lineage and doctrines. Christ was the head of every church.

When examining our family trees today, we investigate by looking first at our parents and then we move on to our grandparents, next our great-grandparents. We continue this process as far as the paper trail will take us. If we had the ability, we would end up in the

Garden of Eden with Adam and Eve as our source. Sometimes, when we have gone as far as our human resources will take us, our last examination is a DNA test. This test will tell us about our ethnic origins.

In the evidence of our connection to the church birthed by Jesus during His earthly ministry, something similar happens. First, we look at the parent church that gave authority for our organizing into an independent church of Christ. Next, we look at the church that birthed our parents, (the grand-parents,) then we move on to their parents, (the great grand-parents.) Like our earthly search for our personal ancestry, we follow a paper trail. Historically, we search for proof of churches that claimed an origin to the original church. In the final analysis, we look at the doctrines and practices of those churches under consideration.

Understanding the need to find a historical link is important in our search to find the bride of Christ today. Logical thinking would tell us that not all "Christian" organizations could identify as the church Jesus proposed to and made His bride during His earthly ministry. Looking at the list of "church" names mentioned above, it is easy to conclude these groups are very doctrinally diverse! Even if we didn't conduct an ancestral search to find a connection to the first church in Jerusalem, a doctrinal search would settle the issue. They could not all be the same as that first church. Some believe we must work for our salvation while others believe it is solely by grace and faith. Some believe that baptism is by sprinkling while, on the other hand, some believe it's by complete immersion. Some believe in intercession to God through Mary and others through Jesus. Hell is contested as a real place of punishment with it just being the grave. Is there a place called purgatory? Can we be baptized for the dead? Is salvation secure? Can it be lost, or is it eternal? Will all the saved be in the bride of Christ or just those who were obedient and faithful to Christ? There are so many questions when we begin looking at the doctrinal beliefs of all who claim to be Christian.

An examination of those first-century churches reveals some doctrinal differences starting to develop even at the end of the apostolic age. They were not as diverse at that time as they are today but still significant enough that Jesus was not going to remain engaged to groups who were believing and teaching things contrary to Him. One of the reasons people get engaged before they marry is to have time to discover if they are compatible in their thinking and lifestyles. It is a time to see if their love for each other can be a full commitment.

Doctrinal error started to develop in the first century Christian churches. The problems began with lessening the demand for repentance and faith. There was an emphasis on external signs and symbols. Some believed that the outward symbols could take the place of inward grace. The greatest departure from doctrinal truth came with the teaching of baptismal regeneration. The churches who were remaining doctrinally true to Christ rejected these churches and ceased fellowship.

There was also a gravitation of some churches toward *episcopacy,* (pastors of larger churches ruling over pastors of smaller congregations.) These churches had moved away from the simplicity of democratic rule in the church as well. In 325 A.D. Constantine called for a gathering of all churches, it has been named the Council of Nicaea. At this meeting, a hierarchy was formed, which rapidly developed into the establishment of the Roman Catholic Church. Constantine called it the *"Universal (Catholic) Church,"* of which he declared himself head. This was the first government-sponsored church, those involved in it became the nucleus of this new doctrinally unsound church. This did not happen overnight! This drifting had been developing for over 200 years. When this church was organized, Constantine declared himself to be the *"head of the church,"* this in itself revealed how far away from God's truth these churches had gone. There is only one *Head of the Church:*

> *For by him were all things created, that are in heaven, and that are in earth, visible and invisible, whether they be thrones, or dominions, or principalities, or powers: all things were created by him, and for him: And he is before all things, and by him all things consist. And he is the head of the body, the church: who is the beginning, the firstborn from the dead; that in all things he might have the preeminence. For it pleased*

the Father that in him should all fulness dwell;
(Colossians 1:16-19)

The **doctrinal unsoundness** of the Catholic church in 325 A.D. is only the beginning of what she will become. When organized by Constantine, she was not worshiping Mary or images. Transubstantiation was not yet imagined. There was no pope and the idea of a person being infallible was not yet developed. *"Immaculate Conception"* (the doctrine that Mary was conceived without original sin,) was not contrived until 1854. Somewhere in the 12th century, the doctrine of purgatory was invented. Much time could be spent revealing the unbiblical practices of the Catholic Church but the main thing to understand is that this conglomerate was not part of Christ's bride. Though there were churches that could show a lineage to the first church, they had been cut off through their doctrinal corruption. This new church had cut off the head of the church (Christ) from the very conception. The head is the mind and all of the body must line up with His thoughts and teaching to be part of His body. Furthermore, the Catholic church, with the power and authority of government killed millions who would not accept her doctrines. Christ loves even heretics and has never given instructions to kill those who do not agree with us.

Once empowered with the authority of the Roman government, the Catholic church began to persecute and kill all who did not agree with them. They were the only authorized church. They even had the ability to enlist Roman soldiers to arrest and kill the Christians of God's true churches.

As mentioned previously, Jesus had not given His church a name. They were known for their lifestyles that were patterned after their Savior and we find a name being given to them by those who lived around them. *Acts, 11:26 "And when he had found him, he brought him unto Antioch. And it came to pass, that a whole year they assembled themselves with the church, and taught much people. And the disciples were called Christians first in Antioch."* Their passion and mission were to preach the gospel and carry out the commands left by Jesus in Matthew 16:18-20. They were not looking for a name to hang out in front of their meeting places.

True churches rejected the newly formed Catholic church and her doctrines. Conflict soon came upon them as converts from the Catholic church were brought into their churches. The Lord's churches did not recognize the baptism administered by this heretical church, thus requiring their new members to be baptized. This infuriated the government church and great persecution and death came to the body of Christ.

Finally, a name was given to the Lord's chosen people. The Catholic church hated these churches and they gave them a derogatory name, the **"Ana-Baptist."** The name meant: **"Re-Baptizers."** God's church did not like this name, they said, "We are not re-baptizing them, we are baptizing them for the first time." God never recognized what the Catholic church was giving as baptism, for they had no authority to be giving it. The issue was not that they were sprinkling or baptizing babies because these practices did not happen until much later in their history. The issue was that they had no authority to baptize, they had been cut off for their doctrinal impurity.

Christ's church was called by different names in different areas and countries, but that *"derogatory"* name Anabaptist remained the catch-all name that stuck with them throughout the persecutions from the Catholics. This name stuck on many of the groups up until the reformation period.

Before I share the many names this *"rose"* was called, let me say that when these names are researched most will have very negative things said of them. They were called heretics and had many false doctrines ascribed to them. We must remember who wrote those histories. These were people who were hiding and struggling to keep their families safe from the onslaught of the government church. They were not writing books about themselves. Rather than their histories being written in books, their history was written in blood. When Jesus promised them that He would protect and preserve them, He told them that the powers of hell would try to destroy them. The hate and terror of the Catholic church empowered by the Roman government tried to wipe their existence out, but God was true to His promise. *Matthew, 16:18 "And I say also unto thee, That thou art Peter, and upon this rock I will build my church; and the gates of hell shall not prevail against it."*

God further promised that He would get glory out of these people who would represent Him and would eventually be the bride of

His Son. *Ephesians, 3:20-21 "Now unto him that is able to do exceeding abundantly above all that we ask or think, according to the power that worketh in us, Unto him be glory in the church by Christ Jesus throughout all ages, world without end. Amen."*

Here are some of their names:

- The Montanist churches often deemed heretics by their enemies were found in Asia Minor.

- The Novation churches were scattered through Italy.

- The Donatist were found in Africa. The Albigensian churches were in France, also in this country, there were   churches called Petrobrusian.

- The Henrician churches were of Switzerland.

- The Arnoldist churches were found in Italy.

- The Berengaria churches were also in France.

- The Waldensian churches were in the Alps and scattered from Rome, Southern France, and as far north as the Netherlands.

- The Anabaptist churches were found in almost every country of Europe, but especially in Bohemia, Moravia, Switzerland and Germany.

Often, many of these other church groups mentioned above would be identified as Anabaptist as well.

- The Paulician churches were in Armenia in the first century and would also be found later in Mesopotamia,   Persia, Taurus mountains as far as Ararat. Many were found along the

Rhine river. The Bogomil sect was found   around

Moscow.

- The Mennonites were scattered throughout Europe.
- The Gazari were in Germany.
- Patterns and Cathari were in Italy.
- The Boni Homines were from Bulgaria.

These are not all of the names given to these faithful Christians who stood for truth and gave their lives for following God's Word. A careful study of church history will reveal many others who died standing for the truth.

These histories are so important in seeing the perpetuating authority given to that first church established in Jerusalem by Jesus Christ. That authority did not end with Christ's death but has continued through the commission given in Matthew 28:18-20. It also continues because of God's promise to that newly established church that the gates of hell would not prevail against her.

Why is the connection to that first church so important? Jesus only engaged Himself to that church He established during His ministry. His promise was to remain the head of the church throughout all ages. His promise in John 14 that He was going to prepare a place for His church that they might live together throughout all eternity is our hope of the eternal ages. We want to be in that bride and live in the New Jerusalem with Him. We do not want to find our residence on the outside of the city. Yes, it does make a difference in what church we serve the Lord.

One of the claims of the Catholic church is that she is the bride of Christ. It is evident from the doctrinal error that brought that church into existence that her claim is false. Not only was she corrupt in her beginning, but she has developed into one of the most doctrinally impure organizations on the face of the earth.

It is interesting to note that in most church history courses in Protestant theological schools, the courses trace their history through this corrupt institution. It is hard to understand why evangelical groups would want to identify themselves with this group. Church history reveals that her power allowed her to kill millions of men, women, and children who would not adhere to her system of doctrines. True churches of Christ have no lineage through the Catholic church. The history of the Anabaptist reveals that these churches were not part of this corrupt church but were the enemies of her. The Catholic church labeled them *"heretics"* and destroyed historical records trying to deny their very existence.

By the reformation period (1500's), the Anabaptist were just being referred to as the Baptist. All of the other names that had been given to her down through the ages had culminated into one. Some were still called Mennonites but most of these started teaching and practicing some things that were unbiblical.

What are we saying then? Are all Baptist churches scriptural and qualify as the espoused bride of Christ? The answer is absolutely not! The largest denomination in the United States is the Catholic church. The name of the next largest group is Baptist. These churches called Baptist are said to be the largest Protestant group in the U.S. There is a problem with this identification, True Baptists have never been Protestants. The term "Protestant" refers to those groups who came out of the Catholic church during the reformation period. The Catholic church called men like Martin Luther, (The founder of the Lutheran church) and others like John Calvin, (founder of the Presbyterian church) "protestors" because they were protesting some of the doctrines of that church. The term Protestant has stuck on most of the churches that have come into existence since the reformation.

As this chapter presents, there has been a lineage from the church that Jesus built in every age. This lineage of churches has connected them back to the authority and doctrines once delivered to the saints by Jesus Himself. Using the Bible as our standard, a very small percentage of the organizations that call themselves Baptist today would qualify as such. What I am saying is that Jesus promised His church they would be here when He returns. Those who have been faithful in their engagement to Christ will be married to Jesus for all eternity:

> Let us be glad and rejoice, and give honour to him: for the marriage of the Lamb is come, and his wife hath made herself ready. And to her was granted that she should be arrayed in fine linen, clean and white: for the fine linen is the righteousness of saints. And he saith unto me, Write, Blessed are they which are called unto the marriage supper of the Lamb. And he saith unto me,

These are the true sayings of God. (Revelation 19:7-9)

Is it a Baptist bride? With the qualification of what a true Baptist church is, my answer would be yes! There may be churches in other parts of the world that go by a different name, but they would have the same lineage that connects them to the authority given by Christ and who are practicing the truths of God's Word. In the next chapter, we will look at some identifying marks and why these marks are necessary to qualify them as part of Christ's espoused bride.

Thirty
She's Not Ecumenical

We live in a religious world that is constantly promoting the idea that all churches and Christian people ought to work together in fellowship meetings, special events, and musical gatherings. To suggest that this is not a good idea will put you in the same class as the Christmas Ogre. Every born again child of God is a brother or sister in Christ and ought to be treated with respect and love but not every child is obedient to Christ's commands. Would this be a problem?

Let's take a logical look at how such an association would work. Without going into long theological discussions on all of the differences existing among organizations that call themselves God's churches, let's consider how it would work. The Catholic church and many Protestant churches believe in the baptism of babies for salvation. Pentecostal churches believe that God's children should speak in a language not known to humans. They also believe that saved children of God can lose their salvation. The Mormons and the Catholic church believe there is an opportunity for salvation after death. The Jehovah Witness' do not believe that Jesus is God. The

Seventh Day Adventist believes we are still under the law. Non-denominational churches don't believe in being dogmatic on doctrines, as long as you are saved that is all that matters. I mention only a few of the doctrinal differences that exist between major Christian organizations, that we might see the folly of ecumenical movements. *Jude, 1:3 "Beloved, when I gave all diligence to write unto you of the common salvation, it was needful for me to write unto you, and exhort you that ye should earnestly contend for the faith which was once delivered unto the saints."*

Be ye not unequally yoked together with unbelievers: for what fellowship hath righteousness with unrighteousness? and what communion hath light with darkness? And what concord hath Christ with Belial? or what part hath he that believeth with an infidel? And what agreement hath the temple of God with idols? for ye are the temple of the living God; as God hath said, I will dwell in them, and walk in them; and I will be their God, and they shall be my people. Wherefore come out from among them, and be ye separate, saith the Lord, and touch not the unclean thing; and I will receive you, And will be a Father unto you, and ye shall be my sons and daughters, saith the Lord Almighty. (2 Corinthians 6:14-18)

The very idea of the church of the Lord Jesus Christ being ecumenical is ridiculous. Throughout the entire ministry of Jesus, He contended with religious leaders who were disobedient to the teachings of God's Word. He became very plain when He spoke with them about their corruption of the commands of God. He loved them and most of the time, He was kind to them but there is never room for man to mess with God's Word.

Two Major Identifiers of the Lord's Church

God, knowing that the onslaught of Satan would be devastating against His church, made sure there would never be a time when her **identity** could not be determined. The enemy who was writing the histories and discrediting the true churches was shrouding the history and perpetuity of this church most of the time. Therefore, God installed within the churches two doctrines that would clearly reveal who they were. These two teachings were made **"laws"** (ordinances) which set them apart from the rest of the doctrines, and they would become the "thorn in the flesh" of all of the counterfeit churches. Those laws are **Baptism** and the **Lord's Supper**. Each of these ordinances has legal distinctions that those who try to copy cannot produce.

Baptism's foundation is plainly seen by the necessity of authority. Only John the Baptist had the authority from God when this law was enacted. The Jewish religious leaders were constantly challenging the authority of John as he established a new act from God contrary to anything the old covenant had demanded of its followers:

And they asked him, What then? Art thou Elias? And he saith, I am not. Art thou that prophet? And he answered, No.

Then said they unto him, Who art thou? that we may

give an answer to them that sent us. What sayest thou

of thyself? He said, I am the voice of one crying in the

wilderness, Make straight the way of the Lord, as said

the prophet Esaias. And they which were sent were of

the Pharisees. (John 1:21-24)

The religious leaders wanted to know, "Who gave you authority to preach and command people to be baptized?"

Jesus, when questioned about His authority to teach and heal people, directed them to this question concerning baptism and who has the authority to administer it:

And when he was come into the temple, the chief priests and the

elders of the people came unto him as he was teaching,

and said, By what authority doest thou these things?

and who gave thee this authority? And Jesus answered

and said unto them, I also will ask you one thing, which

if ye tell me, I in like wise will tell you by what authority

I do these things. The baptism of John, whence was it?

from heaven, or of men? And they reasoned with

themselves, saying, If we shall say, From heaven; he

will say unto us, Why did ye not then believe him? But if

we shall say, Of men; we fear the people; for all hold

John as a prophet. And they answered Jesus, and said,

We cannot tell. And he said unto them, Neither tell I

you by what authority I do these things. (Matthew
21:23-27)

Jesus knew that the authority behind baptism would leave these religious hypocrites without an answer concerning who they were in God's sight.

The doctrine of baptism and the necessity of authority is doing the same thing today to churches who want to claim that they are the chosen people of God. The Catholic church claims to have the authority going back to Peter and claims him as their first pope. Their problem is, they can't get any further back than the head of their church Emperor Constantine who birthed them into existence in 325 A.D. Protestant churches deny the need for authority in baptism knowing they fight a losing battle on that front as the mother church can't provide legitimate authority back to Christ.

Some Baptist churches that can show a historical link have changed doctrinally over the years, denying the need for authority because it would close the door on them from accepting alien baptism. What do I mean by alien baptism? The practice of accepting new members into their churches who have been baptized without proper authority or improperly—; i.e. recognizing infant baptism as acceptable, sprinkling or pouring as satisfactory methods of baptism, or acknowledging baptisms from Catholic or Protestant organizations. Willingness to compromise opens the door for candidates to join their churches without proper baptism. Accepting candidates without the proper authority and mode would remove a restriction that would allow them to increase the size of their congregations. *Matthew, 7:13-14, "Enter ye in at the strait gate: for wide is the gate, and broad is the way, that leadeth to destruction, and many there be which go in thereat: Because strait is the gate, and narrow is the way, which leadeth unto life, and few there be that find it."*

A careful examination of any church that claims to be scriptural in their origin and biblical practices will reveal them as true or false when you discover their position on the doctrine of authority in baptism. True churches will require that any candidate for church membership will first have a testimony of being born again and secondly have baptism from a church qualified to administer it, or be willing to receive it from that church. When considering whether a church meets the qualifications of the New Testament, there are many doctrines that we would examine but if they don't have baptism right, you can move on with your search.

The Lord's Supper is the next doctrine that separates the Lord's churches from the counterfeit. The Catholic church took this doctrine and made it their own. No doubt Satan, realizing the importance of this distinguishing doctrine, made sure his church messed it up as much as possible. They teach that the elements of the supper change when one takes it and this is called *"transubstantiation"* (the change by which the bread and the wine offered in the celebration of the sacrament of the Eucharist becomes, in reality, the body and blood of Jesus Christ.)

"The Eucharist also strengthens the individual because in it Jesus himself, the Word made flesh, forgives our venial sins and gives us the strength to resist mortal sin. It is also the **very channel of eternal life**: Jesus himself. Because of the gravity of Jesus' teaching on receiving the Eucharist, the Catholic Church encourages Catholics to receive frequent Communion, even daily Communion if possible, and mandates the reception of the Eucharist at least once a year during the Easter season." http://www.catholic.com/tracts/who-can-receive-communion. (Information in quotes from the Catholic Answers page. The bold type is mine.)

Therefore, we see that the Catholic church made the Lord's Supper a sacrament that gives saving power. They made it part of their works for salvation teachings. They are not alone in the religious world, there are other groups who also believe that the Lord's Supper has the ability to keep you out of hell. Just as baptism has nothing to do with being born again into the family of God, the Lord's supper, likewise, has nothing to do with getting a person into heaven.

Jesus initiated this supper first with the church He had formed during His earthly ministry. He gathered the apostles, (His church), into the upper room, revealing this beautiful new ordinance, (law), for the first time. Like baptism, this law was new to the Jewish worship. It was instituted while the church was still under the law covenant made with Israel. It was an all Jewish church at this time, as the law would not be fulfilled until the payment for sin was made on the cross.

Colossians, 2:14 "Blotting out the handwriting of ordinances that was against us, which was contrary to us, and took it out of the way, nailing it to his cross." After the death of Jesus and the response of the church to go into all the world, God allowed both Jews and Gentiles to become part of it. Local, independent churches still observed the supper but they restricted it to only members in good standing.

This is where the defining difference in the ordinance makes it a distinguishing mark. Only faithful members of local congregations can take the supper. It is **"closed"** to anyone attending the service that is not a member of that specific church. The qualification for taking the supper isn't, "Are you saved?" It is, "Are you saved, baptized, and a faithful member of the body taking the supper." A church of the Lord wouldn't practice, **"open communion"** allowing all saved people to take the supper. No doubt one of the reasons God made this ordinance closed was because He knew that counterfeit churches would not adopt such a doctrine, as it would be offensive to people and would hinder them from growing to larger sizes. The issue of perpetuating authority is again connected to churches that have historically held these doctrines that made them different from the others.

The Lord's Supper is one of the most beautiful and significant doctrines of the Bible. It is the picture left by the bridegroom (Christ) with His fiancée (the church) to be viewed in every age until His return for the marriage. It was given to the church to remember His death until He returns. The elements of the supper picture more than the deliverance of the saved from hell. The blood shed by the bridegroom for His church is being considered. *Acts, 20:28 "Take heed therefore unto yourselves, and to all the flock, over the which the Holy Ghost hath made you overseers, to **feed the church of God, which he hath purchased with his own blood.**"* This doesn't mean that the blood that was shed for the remission of our sins is not also being considered. Before one can be baptized and become a member of the Lord's church, it is necessary to have a testimony of being born again by the blood of the Lamb. The significance of the cup is that it is being offered only in the church capacity. New Testament examples only reveal the supper happening when the church is gathered together. Remembering again that the word "church" is never used as a term describing all the saved. It always refers to local, visible, congregations.

Furthermore, the broken bread is a picture of His body broken, that His churches might be all over the world. While Jesus was here on earth with His church, the church could only be where Jesus was physically located. Jesus told His church that it was necessary for Him to depart that the Holy Spirit might come and empower churches around the world. *John, 16:7-8 "Nevertheless I tell you the truth; It is expedient for you that I go away: for if I go not away, the Comforter will not come unto you; but if I depart, I will send him unto you. And when he is come, he will reprove the world of sin, and of righteousness, and of judgment:"* Jesus told His church that it was

"expedient" for Him to be crucified and leave them. The meaning of expedient is;: it's necessary to complete a transaction. If He did not leave this world, the church He had established could only be where Jesus was physically. In these scriptures, He promises the Holy Spirit would come upon them and be their comforter and the life force of them. This was not only true for this first church but when the baptism of the Holy Spirit came upon the church at Pentecost, it would continue in them as new churches were organized. Jesus revealed this in *Acts, 1:8 "But ye shall receive power, after that the Holy Ghost is come upon you: and ye shall be witnesses unto me both in Jerusalem, and in all Judaea, and in Samaria, and unto the uttermost part of the earth."*

Jesus is the head, (the mind) of every true church that has propagated from that first church. *Colossians, 1:17-19 "And he is before all things, and by him all things consist. And he is **the head of the body, the church**: who is the beginning, the firstborn from the dead; that in all things he might have the preeminence. For it pleased the Father that in him should all fulness dwell;"* When we eat the bread broken at the Lord's Supper, it is not only significant in revealing how abused Christ's body was on the cross, but it is revealing to His bride that because His body was broken, we can have espoused churches in locations all around the world.

The reason the Lord's Supper needed to be restricted to only members of the local church was for an examination of our relationship with the One to whom we are engaged. God teaches us that discipline of unruly members in the church is necessary to keep the engaged body separated from sin. *Ephesians, 5:25-27, "Husbands, love your wives, even as Christ also loved the church, and gave himself for it; That he might sanctify and cleanse it with the washing of water by the word, that he might present it to himself a glorious church, not having spot, or wrinkle, or any such thing; but that it should be holy and without blemish."*

We see an example of the need for discipline in the Corinthian church where it was allowing a member to live in sin without exercising correction:

> *It is reported commonly that there is fornication among you, and such fornication as is not so much as named among the Gentiles, that one should have his father's wife. And ye are puffed up, and have not rather mourned, that he that hath done this deed might be taken away from among you. For I verily, as absent in body, but present in spirit, have judged already, as though I were present, concerning him that hath so done this deed, In the name of our Lord Jesus Christ, when ye are gathered together, and my spirit, with the power of our Lord Jesus Christ, To deliver such an one unto Satan for the destruction of the flesh, that the spirit may be saved in the day of the Lord Jesus. Your glorying is not good. Know ye not that a little leaven leaveneth the whole*

lump? (1 Corinthians 5:1-6)

The church was instructed to exclude that man to keep the body pure.

Furthermore, they are instructed not to take the Lord's Supper with any who are practicing sin. *1 Corinthians, 5:11, " But now I have written unto you not to keep company, if any man that is called a brother be a fornicator, or covetous, or an idolater, or a railer, or a drunkard, or an extortioner;* **with such an one no not to eat.** *"* He's not talking about not inviting an excluded member over for dinner. Quite the contrary, we are taught to love and encourage erring brothers and sisters in Christ to encourage them to come back. The instruction to the church is to not take the Lord's Supper with those practicing sin.

It is important to understand the supper is a picture for the church. The importance of the picture applies only in reference to the relationship of Christ to His bride:

For I have received of the Lord that which also I delivered unto you, That the Lord Jesus the same night in which he was betrayed took bread: And when he had given thanks, he brake it, and said, Take, eat: this is my body, which is broken for you: this do in remembrance of me. After the same manner also he took the cup, when he had supped, saying, This cup is the new testament in my blood: this do ye, as oft as ye drink it, in remembrance of me. For as often as ye eat this bread, and drink this cup, ye do shew the Lord's death till he come (1 Corinthians, 11:23-26). In these scriptures, the church in Corinth is being instructed about how and why to take the supper. They had been in error in the manner in which they were taking it and the result was sickness and death. *1 Corinthians, 11:30 "For this cause many are weak and sickly among you, and many sleep."* It is clear from this scripture that this ordinance is not to be taken lightly.

The eleventh chapter of Corinthians presents the correct guidelines for taking the supper but one thing stands abundantly clear, there cannot be division in the body of Christ, (the church). The supper was not to be taken when division doctrinally or personally was unrepented of. The rules of this ordinance couldn't be adhered to anywhere but in a local congregation. Furthermore, it could only be enforced upon those who were members.

The Supper is a bridal ordinance because it is a time of examining our relationship with the bridegroom. A man who is engaged to marry a woman and is taking a far journey does not leave His picture with several women—only with His espoused. While he is away at night, she takes the picture out and thinks about him and how much she misses him. Her desire is to be faithful to him and keep herself for him only. When she looks at the picture, if there is anything she has done that might not honor him, she is reminded to remove or repair those things that would hinder the marriage from happening when he returns. We, likewise, take this picture out— looking at our beloved bridegroom, we examine ourselves to see if we love Him with all of our heart and all of our being. It is a time of cleansing and renewing for both the church and the individual members and a time to grow closer in our union with Christ.

God's churches practice this ordinance with the restriction that only members of their particular church can participate in the supper. Why do we do this? Not because it is a great way to grow churches numerically. We practice it this way because it is what the Bible teaches. We practice it this way because the lineage of God's churches has preserved this doctrine for us.

As stated in the beginning of this chapter, God set some clear laws in the New Testament that would be identifiers of His true churches. The obscuring by the enemy could make tracing the history of God's churches difficult. God, knowing this would happen installed two doctrines in His church that would stick out like sore thumbs. He made them easy to identify because the false churches would not want to have anything to do with them. The good news is that His promise that the gates of hell would not prevail against her still prevails today. True churches can still be found around the world holding to the precious doctrines left by Jesus with His church. *Ephesians, 3:20-21 "Now unto him that is able to do exceeding abundantly above all that we ask or think, according to the power that worketh in us, Unto him be glory in the church by Christ Jesus throughout all ages, world without end. Amen."*

Thirty-One

The High Calling of God

Conclusion

Philippians, 3:14 "I press toward the mark for the prize of the high calling of God in Christ Jesus." The encouragement of this book has been to take a look at the eternal ages and the things God has in store for His children who love and serve Him. God's call for men, women, and children is for a commitment that is set on a high standard. We have looked at the **"High Calling"** throughout this book and have understood that God wants the very best for His children. Because He is the *"Best Parent,"* He has set opportunities before us that will motivate and move us to the highest levels of Christianity.

It has been clear from the outset of this book that the *High Calling of God* has been in Christ Jesus. It began with our birth into God's family by our faith in Jesus Christ. We received that gift without providing any works of righteousness on our part. Our salvation has been kept secure in Christ and has never depended on any good works from us. The ability to attain unto higher levels of service has been based completely in Christ. When we have produced works of righteousness, they have been accomplished through our faith in

Christ.

We have understood from the beginning that we are sinners by nature; therefore, our natural tendencies have been our enemy. We became new creatures at the very moment of our faith in Jesus and our entrance into God's family. This has been the source of the righteous works that we have been allowed to produce. Through Christ, our works have been received and acknowledged by God.

Our entrance into the body of Christ, His church, made it possible for us to produce good works by the leadership of the Holy Spirit. Outside of His church, we would not have been able to produce acceptable and satisfactory works . To qualify for production of works, it was necessary to do it through His body the church. We first had to be obedient to His commands. We followed the Lord in baptism and became part of His church. We learned that obedience to God's commands are the only way we can please God and ultimately receive the "prize" of being in the bride of Christ. *2 Timothy, 2:5 "And if a man also strive for masteries, yet is he not crowned, except he strive lawfully."*

The desire of the writer is that those who have read this book now understand what the *"Big Deal"* is about seeking to win the *"prize"* of being in the bride of Jesus. Even though not much is said in the religious world about it, and sometimes miss-information is presented, hopefully, we now see there is a goal worth seeking.

It is hoped that the idea of everyone having the same things in heaven has been dispelled by the clear teachings of the New Testament. All born again believers will not live in the New Jerusalem. Not all will walk on those streets of gold or eat the fruit from the tree of life. While some may conclude that these things are not important, my hope is that the information shared in this book will remove such opinions.

The religious world has come to some conclusions about heaven that just are not biblical concerning what heaven is like. For this reason, the chapter on "Puffy Clouds" was written. Heaven is NOT going to be a boring place with not much to do. We understand that God is the Creator of color, art, and intellectual stimulation, and we are not surprised to find an abundance of all of these stimuli in the eternal ages.

Possibly, one of the biggest shocks to some of the readers is the existence of nations that will be part of the eternal ages. These nations will have a governmental order with kings being the head administrators of them. Also, the realization that even though there will be dwelling places outside of the New Jerusalem, these are described as mansions. There will be no ghetto in the eternal ages. There won't be any gold streets, but the environment will be very pleasing. All of the inhabitants of these nations will be blood-bought children of God living in their new glorified bodies. There will be no night in the new heavens and the light will come from Jesus to the entire world. Outer darkness will not have a place anywhere in the new heaven and new earth.

Two positions are described in the Scriptures that reveal the opportunity for future rewards. The life of the *"overcomer"* which encourages us that God can give us stamina that will resist the Devil and the influences of the world. The promises to the overcomers are so amazing that we ought to seek God for the strength to be known as such. The other position to be desired is that of the disciple who will "pick up his or her cross" and follow the Lord. This represents the child of God who will be willing to suffer with and for Jesus. We would not seek this position because it will produce the easiest life but because it gives the opportunity to be "Christ-like" (Christian.)
My greatest desire in writing this book is to open a view of eternity that would make all of God's children desire to be a "joint heir" with Jesus. The idea of the joint-heir is to share in all of the possessions of Christ—like a husband and wife who share their earthly possessions in "joint tenancy." The bride will be living with Jesus in the eternal ages in the mansion He has prepared for her, being with Him every day experiencing His intellect, guidance, and amazing love. I want to be a part of His Bride, and I am encouraged to make greater commitments in my service to Him. I hope you also, will be encouraged in this way and that this book will be a blessing to you!

Acknowledgments

The *High Calling of God* began for me in 1959 when Jesus Christ converted a lost sinner into one of His children. When we consider acknowledgments, we realize that as sinners, we have little worth but as Paul stated in Philippians 4:13. *"I can do all things through Christ which strengtheneth me."* Without Jesus, this book would not have been written. I acknowledge Him as my strength.

It was 1959. I was attending a non-denominational church, and it was the first time I had ever heard the gospel message preached. The group I was in sent several young people to a camp in August of that summer, and I was one of them. On Friday night, the last night of camp, I received Jesus Christ as my Savior. That changed my life as nothing else has ever done.

In 1965, my wife and I moved from Iowa to California and several months later started attending a small Baptist mission. Before we started visiting, we were not following God like we knew we should. I had become very backslidden, and God was convicting me. One Sunday afternoon, I was with my brother-in-law driving to a place where we could play pool and have a few beers. He was trying to find some music on the radio and hit a station where a preacher was preaching hard on our need for Jesus as a Savior. My sister's husband said to me, "That's a bunch of baloney." I couldn't keep silent, I told him, "I'm the last person in the world to be saying anything about this, but that's not baloney." I was ashamed of my life and knew that I couldn't even share the gospel with my family because of how I was living. That night, I wept in my bed as I prayed to God repenting of my sinful life. I asked God to show me where I could serve Him.

At that time, I was a service plumber and the next morning as I was driving to a plumbing call, I passed a small storefront building that said there was a Baptist mission group meeting there. I went home excited that night and told my wife Linda that I wanted us to attend there on Sunday. We did attend but something happened that made me think we had not found the right church. After morning services, I saw some of the members outside lighting up cigarettes and smoking in the parking area. I went home disappointed.

The next night the Missionary, Ora Holloway showed up at our front door for a visit. I invited him in and as soon as he was seated, I let him know how saddened I was over what I had seen after the services. I told him that the church I attended when I was saved taught that smoking was a sin. I had stopped going to church, and I was convicted about my lifestyle which included smoking. I let him know I was not looking for a "worldly church."

He quickly let me know that he too believed that smoking was a sin, and he didn't do it but there were some at the mission who didn't think it wrong. In our proceeding conversation, he began to share with me some of the truths about being a part of the bride of Christ. Some of the same things that I have presented in this book. I was very interested in what he was sharing; I had never heard these things before. Our conversation went on for some time, and I became frustrated not being able to refute what he was teaching. About 10:30 pm, I finally asked him to go home. I was still upset about the smoking issue, and I let him know that as he was leaving. He was already on the front porch of my house when he turned and said something to me that I will never forget. He looked at me and said, "Brother Wharton, I would rather die with a cigarette in my mouth and be in the bride of Christ, than to have never smoked one and miss out on it." I had to get the last word in as I dismissed him, saying, "I don't think there will be anyone in the bride who smokes anyway!"

God used the missionary's final words to work in my mind and heart for the next couple days. I couldn't get his final statement out of my mind. Finally, I told my wife Linda, "I'm not sure if they are right on the bride issue but if they are, I don't want to miss out on it." We became members of the mission group that week. For several weeks, I would go home and study the Bible trying to prove that some of the things they were teaching were wrong. I remember the day the lights came on in my mind. I was studying, trying to prove them wrong when the Holy Spirit made the Scriptures come alive, it seemed so simple. I saw the harmony of the Scriptures on this subject as well as some others that I had not been able to understand. I must acknowledge Missionary/Pastor Ora Holloway who first cared enough about my family to share the great truths concerning the bride of Jesus.

I acknowledge the many men and women who have shared God's

truth with me down through the years. I am thankful for the seminaries that have helped me and taught me how to study God's Word.

I further acknowledge that without the constant encouragement and help of all who assisted me, this book would not be here today! Finally, where would I be without my beautiful wife Linda? For the past 54 years, she has been my support in anything I have attempted, this book is no exception.

About The Author

I began my early life on a farm in Iowa living with my grandparents. I learned the meaning of hard work living on a farm, not only because of the agricultural work but because my grandfather also owned a plumbing business. We would rise early, milk cows, eat breakfast and then load the plumbing truck with the equipment needed for the days work. Arriving home in the later afternoon, those silly cows wanted to be milked again. I am thankful for the work ethic I learned in the state of Iowa.

In 1962, I married my high school sweetheart, Linda. We were married on a Saturday night, and I went to work as an apprentice plumber on Monday morning. There was no money for a honeymoon, but we were young, in love and it all seemed good to us.

When my wife married me, I was a plumber but not long after, she got a big surprise. In 1965 I surrendered to the call of God to preach His Word. I attended seminary at Fresno Missionary Baptist Institute, in Fresno, Ca. receiving my Bachelor of Theology degree. My Master of Arts in Biblical Counseling was attained at Shasta Bible College, in Redding, Ca. God has used me for the past 50 years pastoring churches in California. For health reasons, it was necessary for me to retire in 2014.

I still love preaching and teaching and remain active in the ministry. Occasionally, I am invited to present seminars on God's preservation of the King James Bible. God has opened a new ministry for me this past year in the arena of writing. I have written a fiction novel called the Cabbie and now I present my first doctrinal book. I am excited about this new ministry and hope to be sharing new books with you in the future.

Made in the USA
Middletown, DE
14 August 2023

36715887R00146